INSPIRAT...

ALONG   THE   HOMELESS

TRAIL

INSPIRATIONAL POEMS
FOR ALL SEASONS AND REASONS

WALTER ELLIS III

This book is dedicated to the memories of my
Dear sweet mother Bessie Ellis
Who taught me to live by this motto?

If only I can help one somebody maybe my life
Will not be lived in vain

THANKS TO ALL MY
FAMILY AND
FRIENDS

PREFACE

ALONG THE HOMELESS TRAIL HAS BEEN WRITTEN FOR CHILDREN AND ADULTS OF ALL AGES WITH THE HOPE AND POSSIBILITY THAT ONE DAY SOMEONE WILL BE INSPIRED TO HELP SOMEONE ELSE ALONG THE ROAD OF LIFE WE ALL MUST TRAVEL *CHILDREN* AND ADULTS ALIKE WE ARE ALL LONGING TO BELONG TO SOMETHING NO ONE WANTS TO BE ALONE MOST OF US WANT AND NEED CONFIRMATION FROM OUR PARENTS SPOUSES CHURCH OR COMMUNITY THE COLLECTION OF POEMS WRITTEN IN THIS BOOK WILL GIVE INSPIRATION TO SOME EDUCATE OTHERS AND ENTERTAIN ALL OF IT'S READERS AFTER YEARS OF DRUG AND ALCOHOL ABUSE AND DEPRESSION I WAS DETERMINED TO CHANGE MY LIFE AND BECOME A PRODUCTIVE MEMBER OF SOCIETY IN AND OUT OF TREATMENT FACILITIES AND IN AND OUT OF HOMELESS SHELTERS I WENT THEN ONE DAY IN JANUARY 1996 I WROTE A POEM ENTITLED **SURFACE** IT FILL ME WITH INSPIRATION EVERY TIME I READ IT I BEGAN TO CHANGE THE WAY I LOOKED AT LIFE LIVING IN A HOMELESS SHELTER WASN'T EASY THE PEOPLE AROUND ME ENJOYED READING MY POEMS SO I CONTINUE TO WRITE THEM BY THE MONTH OF JUNE 1996 TO MY AMAZEMENT I HAD WRITTEN ONE HUNDRED AND TWENTY FOUR OF THEM MOST OF THEM ARE WRITTEN FROM MY PERSONAL BELIEFS SOME OF THEM ARE PURELY ENTERTAINING AND ALL OF THEM ARE FROM MY HEART I PRAY THAT READING THIS BOOK WILL BE DELIGHTFUL AND HELPFUL

TO ALL

TABLE OF CONTENT
HUMANISTIC

RELIGIOUS

RECOVERY

CAPTIVATION

OCCASION

SURFACE

SOMETIMES I DIG DEEP INTO MY MIND

TO FIND THAT PERSON WHO'S CARING AND KIND

ONLY YOU KNOW WHERE TO LOOK AND FIND

THAT PERSON YOU HAVE BURIED DEEP INSIDE

ONCE YOU HAVE FOUND THEM RELEASE THEM OUTSIDE

THEN LET YOU HIGHER POWER BE YOUR GUIDE AND SURFACE

WHY ME

WHEN YOU ARE TIRED AND YOU FEEL THAT YOU HAVE

DONE YOUR BEST THEN PEOPLE AROUND YOU

COMPLAIN AND CONTINUE TO START UP THE MESS

PUTTING YOU DOWN AND MAKING YOU FEEL ASHAMED

DON'T FEED INTO IT AND WORRY IF YOU ARE TO BLAME

JUST TAKE IT TO GOD AND ASK FOR HIS HELP

THEN GOD WILL LEAD YOUR EVERY STEP

YOU SHOULD FEEL A RELEASE DEEP INSIDE

KNOWING THAT NO ONE CAN TAKE AWAY YOUR PRIDE

STAND

WHAT DOES IT TAKE TO BECOME A MAN

SOME OF US CAN'T AND SOME OF US CAN

BEING RESPONSIBLE GETS YOU PART OF THE WAY

YOU HAVE TO LOVE OTHERS DAY BY DAY

LIVING AN HONEST LIFE IS THE BEST WAY TO GO

PRAY TO YOUR GOD HE WILL LET YOU KNOW

WHEN THE TIME COMES YOU CAN MAKE A STAND

THEN PRAISE GOD AND TELL THEM YOU ARE A MAN

ATTENTION

IF YOU DON'T FOCUS LIFE GOES BY FAST

BEFORE YOU KNOW IT THE PRESENT IS THE PAST

TAKING YOUR TIME TO LIVE HONEST AND RIGHT

WILL MAKE LIFE EASIER SO YOU DON'T HAVE TO FIGHT

STAYING AWARE OF WHAT IS GOING ON AROUND YOU

WILL MAKE LIFE BETTER THIS I KNOW IS TRUE

SO DON'T RUSH LIFE LIKE YOU HAVE DONE BEFORE

TAKE YOUR TIME SO GOD CAN HELP YOU MORE

JUST PRAY TO HIM TO SHOW YOU THE WAY

HE WILL MAKE YOUR LIFE TROUBLE FREE EVERYDAY

CONVERSE

IT'S DIFFICULT FOR ME TO COMMUNICATE IN LIFE

TRYING TO SOCIALIZE AND INTERACT WITHOUT

CAUSING STRIFE

LEARNING TO COMMUNICATE IN VARIES SITUATIONS

KNOWING WHEN TO SPEAK AND HOW WITHOUT
CAUSING AGGRAVATION

I MUST HAVE PATIENCE CLOSE MY MOUTH AND

OPEN MY EARS

MOST OF ALL PRAY TO GOD TO REMOVE ALL MY FEARS

TODAY I KNOW TO TAKE MY TIME TO MAKE

MY LIFE COMPLETE

I MUST RESPECT OTHERS AND CARE TO OVERCOME DEFEAT

IT WON'T BE EASY BUT I MUST CONTINUE TO TRY

TO COMMUNICATE WITH THE HELP OF GOD

BEFORE THE DAY I DIE

IT'S
OK
TODAY

THE WORLD WE LIVE IN IS SO FULL OF SIN

RACISM MURDER STEALING BUILDS HATRED WITHIN

BECAUSE OF PEER PRESSURE IT'S BETTER

TO DO THINGS ALONE

IT'S OK NOT TO FOLLOW AND TO BE

A LEADER ON YOUR OWN

DOING THINGS THE RIGHT WAY YOU MAY

THINK YOU'RE ALL ALONE

BUT SOON YOU REALIZE OTHERS

ARE FOLLOWING YOU HOME

SO DON'T BE DISCOURAGE AT ALL IF YOU

ARE NOT AMONG THE IN CROWD

BECAUSE SOON THEY'LL HOPE TO BE LIKE YOU

WALKING HAPPY AND PROUD

HOME

SWEET HOME

FOR YEARS NOW I'VE BEEN ON A HOMELESS TRAIL KNOWING

IT'S MY FAULT NOT PAYING ATTENTION TO DETAILS

LIVING IN SHELTERS HAS HELP ME ALONG THE WAY

BUT I STILL PRAY TO GOD FOR MY OWN HOME TODAY

PEOPLE WITH THE POWER SEEM TO TURN THEIR BACK

NOT HAVING THE COMPASSION TO HELP ME GET ON TRACK

THEY ARE ALWAYS SENDING MILLIONS OVER SEAS

WHILE HOMELESS IN THIS COUNTRY ARE DYING FROM DISEASE

I HAVE HEARD THAT CHARITY STARTS AT HOME

IT SEEMS IN THIS COUNTRY THE HOMELESS STAND ALONE

JOBS AND AFFORDABLE HOUSING WILL BE A START

IF THE PEOPLE IN POWER LOOK DEEP INTO THEIR HEART

TO FIND LOVE THEN SHARE IT WITH GOD IN MIND

THIS SHOULD WORK IF THEY PUT IN THE TIME

I PRAY TO GOD THEY USED THE MONEY WHERE IT BELONG

SO HOMELESS CAN ONE DAY SAY HOME SWEET HOME

TICK

TOCK

MILLIONS OF PEOPLE AROUND THE WORLD

CONSTANTLY ASK THE TIME MAN WOMAN BOY AND GIRL

GOING TO WORK SHOP SCHOOL AND PLAY

SIXTY SECONDS IN A MINUTE LOOKING AT THE

TIME ALL DAY

IF YOU ARE HONEST OPEN MINDED AND WILLING

TO LEARN

YOU WILL KNOW THAT GOD GIVES US THIS TIME AND IT

MUST BE EARNED

USING IT TO DO HIS HOLY WILL SHALL SET YOU FREE

LOVING OTHERS WITH GOD IN MIND YOUR TIME SHOULD BE

DEEP IN YOUR HEART YOU WILL FEEL OH SO FINE

NEVER HAVING TO WONDER AND WORRY ABOUT THE TIME

AS ONE

THE WORLD WE LIVE IN IS SO FULL OF MISERY

IF SOME OF US HAD THE POWER IT WOULD BE OVER

WITH BY THE COUNT OF THREE

BUT THAT'S NOT THE WAY TO MAKE LIFE BETTER

WE MUST PRAY TO GOD AND LOVE EACH OTHER FOREVER

AS A NATION WE ARE SEARCHING IN OUTER SPACE

FOR A NEW HOME

BUT FIRST WE MUST ALL LEARN DOWN HERE

HOW TO GET ALONE

WE MUST HAVE LOVE FOR EACH OTHER AND SPREAD IT

AROUND THE WORLD

PUTTING A SMILING FACE ON EVERY

MAN WOMAN BOY AND GIRL

IF WE DO THIS OUR WORLD WILL BE ONE HAPPY HOME

THEN WHEN WE REACH OUR HOME IN OUTER SPACE

THERE WILL BE NO WRONG

PEACE   WITHIN

DON'T FALL INTO SOMEONE ELSE'S NEGATIVE TRAP

PAY CLOSE ATTENTION DON'T LISTEN TO THEIR

NEGATIVE RAP THEY WILL LEAD YOU TO NEGATIVE REACTION

THAT MIGHT CAUSE YOU TO END UP IN TRACTION

SO WHEN THEIR TONGUE BEGAN TO ROLL

DON'T REACT NEGATIVELY AND LOSE CONTROL

NO ONE CAN MAKE YOU ACT LIKE A FOOL

JUST SMILE AT THEM AND KEEP YOUR COOL

YOU WILL FEEL BETTER KNOWING THEY DIDN'T WIN

THEN BE PROUD OF YOURSELF AND HAVE PEACE WITHIN

LISTEN

BIRDS IN THE AIR AND FISHES IN THE SEA

MEAN MORE TO LIFE THAN YOU THINK THEY SHOULD BE

FLOWERS ON THE GROUND AND STARS IN THE SKY

HAVE SOMETHING TO SAY IF YOU LOOK CLOSELY

WITH YOUR EYES

THE RAIN AND THE CLOUDS EVEN THE SUNSHINE

SHOULD BE PAID ATTENTION TO BY ALL OF MANKIND

THERE'S A LESSON TO BE LEARNED FOR THOSE

FAR AND NEAR

TO THEM WHO HAVE EARS LET THEM HEAR THEN LISTEN

BEST ASSETS

KNOWLEDGE WISDOM AND POWER ARE THREE IMPORTANT ASSETS

YOU CAN'T GET IN AN HOUR KNOWLEDGE CAN BE GAIN

THROUGH HARD WORK EDUCATION AND TIME KNOWLEDGE IN TIME

WILL HELP YOU TO OBTAIN WISDOM IN MIND WISDOM WILL

TAKE YOU FAR IN LIFE JUDGING YOUR WRONG FROM RIGHT

BEING ABLE TO JUDGE HONESTLY WILL PUT POWER INTO

YOUR HANDS IN THIS WORLD WITH POWER YOU CAN BOLDLY

MAKE A STAND WITH ALL OF THESE IN TIME YOU CAN LIVE

LIFE WITH EASE HELPING OTHERS AND THANKING GOD WILL

MAKE HIM PLEASED PRAYING TO HIM FOR THE BLESSING

THAT HE GIVES TO YOU EVERY HOUR KNOWING THROUGH

HIM YOU WILL RECEIVE KNOWLEDGE WISDOM AND POWER

WAITING

ON

PROMISES AND   DREAMS

NOW IS THE TIME TO MAKE UP YOUR MIND

TO DO WHAT IS NEEDED TO BE DONE AT THIS TIME

THE WORLD WE LIVE IN FOR YOU IT WILL NOT WAIT

WAITING ON PROMISES AND DREAMS MIGHT BE TO LATE

SO MY ADVISE TO YOU IF YOU WANT TO MAKE IT THROUGH

GET OFF YOUR BUTT OUT OF THE RUT AND START A NEW

LOOK FOR A JOB AND BE RESPONSIBLE IF YOU KNOW

WHAT THAT MEANS

THEN FORGET ABOUT YESTERDAY WAITING ON

PROMISES AND DREAMS

WHAT'S

UP WITH THAT

IT'S VERY DIFFICULT FOR TEACHERS TO TEACH STUDENTS

WEARING HUNDRED DOLLARS SHOES AND GOLD ARE HARD TO

REACH THE PRESIDENT MAKES MORE IN A DAY THAN

A TEACHER WITH TIME BUT WHO PUT THE THOUGHTS AND THE

KNOWLEDGE INTO THEIR MIND DOCTORS LAWYERS EVEN THE BEST

OF ATHLETES SOMEONE HAD TO SHOW THEM HOW TO STUDY

TO BECOME COMPLETE SO WHY DO TEACHERS GET PAID

SUCH LOW WAGES WHEN THE CAREERS OF THE ONES THEY TEACH

GET PAID OUTRAGEOUS THE PEOPLE IN POWER NEED TO

TAKE A GOOD LOOK WHEN THEY APPROPRIATE THE FUNDS

TO THE ONES WITH THE BOOKS TEACHERS IN THIS COUNTRY

SHOULD GET PAID MORE MONEY BECAUSE

EDUCATING OUR CHILDREN IS NOTHING FUNNY

DEEP

DOWN WITHIN

I MUST LISTEN TO WHAT MY SOUL IS SAYING DAILY ON MY

KNEES TO MY HIGHER POWER I MUST START PRAYING

FOR THE WISDOM TO UNDERSTAND THIS FEELING DEEP INSIDE

THE STRENGTH TO FACE THE TRUTH AND NOT TRY TO

RUN AND HIDE I MUST SURRENDER TO THIS SPIRIT THAT

TELLS ME TO DO RIGHT SO THE LIFE THAT I'M LIVING

CAN ENDURE ANY STRIFE I KNOW THAT'S IT TIME TO RECEIVE

A LIFE WORTH LIVING THEN LISTEN TO MY SOUL

THAT IS LIFE GIVING

NO   VACANCY

STOP ALLOWING OTHERS TO RENT FREE SPACE

IN YOUR HEAD

WORRYING ABOUT HE SAYS AND SHE SAYS AND

WHAT HAS BEEN SAID THE TIME

YOU HAVE SHOULD BE SPENT AS POSITIVE

AS CAN BE

IGNORING THE NEGATIVE AND THE PEOPLE UPON WHICH

THAT IS ALL THEY SEE HAVING A PURE HEART

WITH AN OPEN MIND WILL HELP YOU TO SEE CLEAR

TO RECOGNIZE THE OPPOSITION BEFORE IT

COMES TO NEAR THE MIND IS A TERRIBLE THING TO

WASTE THEY SAY SO DON'T ALLOW ANYONE TO RENT

FREE SPACE IN YOUR HEAD TODAY

BLESSED HOUSE

THERE ONCE WAS A DAY THAT I WAS LOST I LOOKED

TOWARD THE HEAVENS FOR GUIDANCE FROM MY BOSS

JUST LIKE JOSEPH AND MARY LOOKING FOR A PLACE TO LAY

HERE I WAS HOMELESS WITHOUT A PLACE TO STAY

THEN A LIGHT FROM HEAVEN LEAD ME TO THE **HESED**

A SHELTER FOR THE HOMELESS WITH DIRECTORS

THAT ARE THE BLESSED THEY FEED ME CLOTHE ME AND EVEN

LET ME TAKE A BATH ON WEEKENDS THEY SHOW MOVIES

THAT LIFTS MY SPIRITS MAKING ME LAUGH

BEING HERE IS LIKE HAVING A CLOSE AND CARING FAMILY

WITHOUT THEIR LOVE AND CONCERN WHO KNOWS

WHERE I WOULD BE I THANK GOD FOR THE **HESED HOUSE**

A PLACE WHERE THE HOMELESS CAN GO

WITH BROTHERLY LOVE SO STRONG

THE WHOLE WORLD SHOULD KNOW

EENY MEENY MINEY MO

THERE IS SOMETHING YOU MUST PAY STRICT ATTENTION TOO

IF YOU DON'T THE DECISION YOU MAKE MIGHT STOP YOUR

DREAM FROM BECOMING TRUE LIVING IN THIS WORLD TODAY

YOU MUST CHOOSE RIGHT OVER WRONG NOBODY WANTS TO LOSE

THE CHOICE YOU MAKE IN THE MORNING MIGHT KILL

YOU IN THE NIGHT BUT CHOOSING WISELY COULD MAKE YOU

THE RICHEST PERSON IN SIGHT EVERYDAY YOUR BRAIN

COULD MAKE UP TO A MILLION DECISIONS

SOME VOLUNTARY SOME INVOLUNTARY BUT ALWAYS

WITH PRECISION ONCE THE PROCESS IS OVER THEN IT'S ALL

UP TO YOU A DECISION MUST BE MADE ON WHAT YOU ARE

ABOUT TO DO GOD GIVES YOU THE POWER TO CHOOSE TO DO

HIS HOLY WILL WITH THAT POWER YOU CAN RESIST

ALL THE DEVIL'S DEALS CHOOSING USING WISDOM

IS IMPORTANT IN YOUR LIFE YOU SHOULD KNOW A LITTLE MORE

COMPLICATED THAN EENY MEENY MINEY MO

PEACE BE STILL

CLOSE YOUR EYES RELAXING YOUR BODY LISTEN TO YOUR

HEART BEAT LET THE SOUND OF THE OCEAN WAVES RELAX YOU

FROM HEAD TO FEET HEAR THE VOICES OF THE SEA GULLS

WHISPERING IN THE WILD CLEAR YOU'RE MIND OF ALL

NEGATIVE THOUGHTS THINK BACK TO WHEN YOU WERE A CHILD

THE HAPPY TIMES YOU HAD KNOWING THAT GOD WAS

WATCHING OVER YOU THE RAIN AND THE THUNDER RELAXES ME

YOU SHOULD FEEL RELAXED TOO

LET YOUR MIND DRIFT WITH THE RAIN AND THE WIND

HAVING PEACE AND SERENITY COMFORTING YOUR

BODY AND MIND DEEP WITHIN

CONCENTRATE WITH YOUR EYES CLOSED TO SEE

THE SEA GULLS FLYING FEELING THE HEAT OF

THE SUNSHINE WHILE ON THE BEACH YOU ARE LYING

KNOWING WITHIN YOUR HEART YOU ARE ABLE TO DO

GOD'S WILL ENJOYING THE REST OF YOUR LIFE SAYING

PEACE BE STILL

DING   DING   DING

THERE ONCE WAS A TIME WHEN I WAS A CHILD

I HEARD A SIREN AND THEN A BELL THAT MADE ME SMILE

WHEN I LOOKED UP THERE BEFORE MY EYES A BIG RED

FIRE TRUCK YOU SHOULD HAVE SEEN THE SIZE THERE ON TOP

OF THE TRUCK A DOG SAT WITH SPOTS BLACK AND WHITE

WITH ALL THE EXCITEMENT I SAID TO MYSELF OH WHAT A

SIGHT NOW THAT I AM OLDER I STILL FEEL THE SAME

WHENEVER I HEAR THAT SIREN I STOP AND LISTEN

FOR THE BELL TO RING I LOVE FIRE TRUCKS SO MUCH

I LIKE TO HAVE THEM ALL AROUND

IF SOMETHING EVER HAPPEN TO THEM I WOULD SURELY

WEAR A FROWN IF I EVER GET THE CHANCE I WILL MAKE

THE BELL RING OH HOW HAPPY I WOULD BE TO HEAR THE SOUND

DING DING DING

HOMELESS TRAIL

AS I AWAKE IT'S FIVE THIRTY IN THE MORNING TIME TO

CLEAR MY MIND HOPING AND PRAYING TO GOD THAT

HE BLESSES MY DAY WITH LOTS OF SUNSHINE ON THE TRAIL

TO BREAKFAST A COUPLE OF MILES I MUST GO

IT WOULD BE NICE TO MAKE SOME MONEY ALONG THE WAY

YOU KNOW BACK ON THE TRAIL AFTER BREAKFAST TO LUNCH

A COUPLE OF MILES TO PORT ON THE WAY I STILL PRAY

FOR A HUSTLE THAT WON'T HAVE ME GOING TO COURT AFTER

GOD HAS BLESSED ME WITH A TWO HOUR JOB THAT'S NOT

VERY HARD THEN IT'S ON THE TRAIL A FEW MILES BACK

TO WHERE THIS MORNING I STARTED AFTER A SHOWER A

LITTLE T.V. AND FOOD IT'S OFF TO BED BEFORE I SLEEP

I THANK GOD FOR A PLACE TO LAY MY HEAD MORNING COMES

QUICK THE LIGHTS ARE ON SOON OUT THEY WILL SEND I

THANK YOU GOD FOR ANOTHER SUNNY DAY

I'M ON THE HOMELESS TRAIL AGAIN

DOWN

BUT   NOT

OUT

THERE MAY COME A TIME IN YOUR LIFE YOU WILL FEEL

LONELY AND LOST IN DESPAIR YOUR HEART WILL ACHE AND YOU

WILL TELL YOURSELF NO ONE IN THE WORLD REALLY CARE

INSTEAD OF CRYING AND WADDLING IN SELF PITY WORRYING

ABOUT THE PROBLEM AT HAND FIND A BIBLE AND OPEN IT

TO PROVERBS READ ABOUT THE GOOD NEWS FOR YOU GOD

HAS ALREADY PLANNED READING THE BIBLE WILL EASE

YOUR HEART ACHE LIFTING YOU OUT OF DESPAIR

YOU WILL KNOW WHATEVER THE PROBLEM GOD WILL BE THERE

AND THAT HE REALLY DOES CARE YOUR PROBLEM WILL

DISAPPEAR AND YOUR BURDENS WILL BE LIGHT

THEN THANK GOD FOR THE POWER TO STAND UP AND

THE WILL TO WIN THE FIGHT

THE   HOOD

GROWING UP IN THE HOOD USED TO BE ALL RIGHT THE WORST

THING THAT COULD HAVE HAPPENED TO YOU WAS YOU MIGHT

HAVE GOTTEN INTO A FIGHT NEIGHBORS WERE CONCERNED FOR

ALL THE CHILDREN AROUND ON WEEKENDS YOU COULD GO SEE

A MOVIE AT THE SHOW DOWNTOWN TIMES HAS CHANCE

DRASTICALLY IN THE WAY THE HOOD IS RUN NOW SOME OF THE

CHILDREN ALREADY KNOW HOW TO USE A GUN GANGS HAVE

BECOME POPULAR REPLACING THE LOCAL BOY SCOUTS IT'S

THE NORM TO HEAR GUNFIRE AND THE DISTANT SOUNDS

OF SHOUTS LADIES OF THE NIGHT ARE PLENTY

THAT IS WHAT THEY SAY NOT ONLY AT NIGHT BUT YOU

CAN FIND MANY OF THEM IN THE DAY DRUGS ARE RUNNING

RAMPANT EVERY WHICH WAY YOU LOOK PEOPLE ARE DYING

FROM NOT KNOWING WHAT TYPE OF DRUGS THEY TOOK PEOPLE

NEED TO MAKE A CHANGE OH HOW I WISH

THEY WOULD SO LIFE WILL BE BETTER WHILE

LIVING IN THE HOOD

23

IMPOSSIBLE DREAM

BLOWING OUT THE CANDLES AND HOPING YOUR WISH

WILL COME TRUE

MOST OF US AS HUMANS RITUALLY BELIEVE

THIS IS THE THING TO DO

A CHILD PUT A TOOTH UNDERNEATH THE PILLOW

BEFORE SLEEPING AT NIGHT

RISING IN THE MORNING TO SEE IF THE TOOTH FAIRY

HAS MADE THE FLIGHT

MOST OF OUR LIVES WE SPEND A LOT OF TIME

WISHING AND NOT GIVING UP HOPE

FOR THE WORLD WE LIVE IN YOU MUST

BELIEVE IN SOMETHING IN ORDER TO COPE

WISHING UPON A FALLING STAR MAY NOT BE

AS FAR FETCHED AS IT SEEMS

IT JUST MIGHT BE YOUR TURN IN LIFE TO RECEIVE THAT

IMPOSSIBLE DREAM

BEFORE

YOU'RE

OLD

THE WINDS OF TIME HAS CHANGED MY SIGN

BLOWING ME INTO THIS STATE OF MIND

CONSCIOUSLY CARING WITH LOVE AND CONCERN

THIS IS A LESSON THAT WE ALL MUST LEARN

THIS WORLD CONTINUES TO TURN AROUND AND AROUND

WAITING FOR NO ONE TO GET THEIR FEET ON THE GROUND

WINTER SPRING SUMMER AND FALL ARE THE SEASONS

JUST RECOGNIZE THEM DON'T LOOK FOR A REASON

TIME WILL HEAL YOUR MIND BODY AND SOUL

YOU MUST SUBMIT TO IT ALL BEFORE YOU'RE OLD

SPACE AND TIME

CLOSE YOUR EYES AND RELAX LET YOUR THOUGHTS DISSIPATE

CONCENTRATE ON THE SOUNDS OF THE OCEAN ALLOW YOUR

BODY AND MIND TO RELATE LISTEN AS THE CALMING EFFECT

OF THE RUSHING WATERS SOOTHES YOUR INNER SOUL THE

FEELING OF PEACE AND TRANQUILLITY ENGULFS YOU LIKE

RIDING IN A CONVERTIBLE ON THE OPEN ROAD

AS THE BEAT OF YOUR HEART SLOWS DOWN

TO A SERENE GENTLE RELAXING RATE

YOU ARE DRIFTING OFF OH SO SLOWLY INTO

A HYPNOTIC SLEEPY TRANSCENDENTAL STATE

LET THE WATERS EASE ALL THE TENSION THROUGHOUT

YOUR BODY SLOWLY CARESSING YOUR MIND

FLOW WITH THE FEELING AS YOUR BODY

STARTS TO GO LIMP YOUR MIND FLOATS INTO SPACE AND TIME

FLOAT FLOAT FLOAT INTO THE SPACE IN YOUR MIND

FLOAT FLOAT FLOAT INTO SPACE AND TIME

26

ONE ACCORD

LOOK UP INTO THE SKY AND BEHOLD IT'S COMING

OUT OF THE EAST

YOU MUST UNDERSTAND FOR THEY ARE HERE

TO SAVE US FROM THE BEAST

IN THESE TROUBLED TIMES YOU MUST

KNOW THE TRUTH

THINK BACK TO THE STORIES YOU HEARD

AS A YOUTH

YOU MUST KNOW FOR YOURSELF THE REASON

THEY ARE HERE

DON'T LISTEN TO THE NUMBERS THAT TELL

YOU TO FEAR

IF YOU BELIEVE AND HAVE FAITH THEN YOU CAN

GET ABOARD

TRUSTING I AM THAT I AM THEN WE'LL BE

ON ONE ACCORD

BETTER

THINK   AGAIN

THROUGHOUT HISTORY ALL OVER THE WORLD PEOPLE HAVE SEEN
U.F.O.S.

THE QUESTION IS WHERE DO THEY COME FROM NOBODY

REALLY KNOWS

IN OUR UNIVERSE THERE ARE MILLIONS OF PLANETS

LIKE THE ONE WE LIVE ON

THERE'S A GOOD POSSIBILITY SOMEWHERE IN OUR UNIVERSE

RIGHT NOW ONE IS BEING BORN

GOD CREATED THIS UNIVERSE WITH ALL OF HIS

INFINITE WISDOM

BEINGS FROM OTHER PLANETS GOD COULD HAVE DECIDED

TO MAKE SOME

HUMANS HAVE TRAVEL INTO OUTER SPACE

YOU REMEMBER WHEN

THERE'S A GOOD POSSIBILITY THERE'S LIFE

OUT THERE IF YOU DON'T THINK SO YOU BETTER THINK AGAIN

UP   IN

SMOKE

FROM THE TIME THAT CAVEMEN DISCOVERED FIRE

THE MISUSE OF IT HAS CAUSE DEATH AND MANY

MEN TO BECOME LIARS TOBACCO HAS GROWN IN THIS

COUNTRY FOR MANY OF YEARS THE MISUSE OF IT HAS

CAUSED DEATH BRINGING MANY PEOPLE TO TEARS SOME SAY

SMOKING CAUSES LUNG CANCER AND CANCER KILLS OTHERS

SAY SMOKING IS OK WHAT IS THE BIG DEAL

IF YOU WANT TO KNOW THE TRUTH GO TO THE HOSPITAL AND

SEE FOR YOURSELF THERE YOU WILL FIND MANY PEOPLE FACED

WITH THE FEAR OF DEATH THE QUESTION IS IN THIS WORLD

TODAY WHO DO YOU BELIEVE I REMEMBER MY DYING MOTHER

SAYING STOP THE SMOKING PLEASE

TIME

PASSES

FEEL THE SUNSHINE ON YOUR BODY LET IT GENERATE

YOUR MIND LET THE RAINDROPS POUR OUT ALL OVER YOU

WITH THE RHYTHM OF TIME THE THUNDER AND LIGHTING

SPEAKS WITH AUTHORITY TRYING TO GET YOU TO HEAR

WITH AN OPEN MIND AND A PURE HEART YOU SHOULD FEEL IT

OH SO CLEAR THE WIND BLOWS AS THE SECONDS OF LIFE

SLOWLY TICS AWAY THE HAIL MAY COME JUST TO LET YOU

KNOW WHAT THEY ARE TRYING TO SAY AS THE SNOW FLAKES FALL

THEY ARE ALL DIFFERENT SHAPES AND SIZE

BY NOW A CHILD WOULD BE ABLE TO SEE IT ALL AND THEN

REALIZE IF YOU WANT TO KNOW WHAT TIME IT IS DON'T

LOOK AT THE CLOCK ON THE WALL

LOOK UP AND AROUND THEN RECOGNIZE WINTER SPRING

SUMMER AND FALL AS TIME PASSES

SHARING

TIME

CHILDREN NEED A LOT OF GUIDANCE IN LIFE

TO HELP THEM GROW IN THE RIGHT WAY WITH ALL

THE JUNK ON TELEVISION WHO KNOWS WHAT THEY

WILL LEARN TODAY IT TAKES A SPECIAL KIND OF CHILD

TO BE WILLING TO GIVE UP THEIR TIME

GOING OUT OF THEIR WAY TO HELP OTHERS

WHILE KEEPING GOD IN MIND LEARNING TO HELP OTHERS

STARTING AT SUCH A YOUNG AGE THEY WILL BECOME

RESPONSIBLE ADULTS NOT BEHAVING CARELESSLY OR OUTRAGED

I'M BLESSED TO HAVE MET SOME STUDENTS WHO WILLING

GAVE THEIR TIME AWAY

HELPING THE HOMELESS AND LEARNING TO SHARE THE LOVE

THEY HAVE EVERYDAY THEIR PARENTS SHOULD

BE PROUD OF THEM THANKING GOD FOR CHILDREN SO KIND

FOR THEY WILL LEARN A VALUABLE LESSON EARLY IN LIFE

BY SHARING TIME

IF
WE   CAN

WHEN GOD FORMED MAN USING THE DUST OF THE GROUND

THERE WERE NO OTHER HUMANS HERE

ONLY GOD'S CREATURES WERE AROUND

HE TOLD MAN TO RULE OVER ALL THE ANIMALS

TO BE FOUND

LIVING IN THE OPEN OUTDOORS CLOSE TO NATURE

IN THE WILD

MAKES YOU FEEL GOOD KNOWING THAT GOD IS

BLESSING YOU ALL THE WHILE

DEALING WITH THE ELEMENTS MAY CAUSE YOU

TO REMEMBER WHEN YOU WERE A CHILD

MAN HAS GOTTEN AWAY SOMEHOW

FROM GOD'S ORIGINAL PLAN

FOR MAN TO LIVE IN HARMONY WITH NATURE AND RULE

WITH A STRONG HAND

I THANK IT TIME FOR MAN TO GET IN TOUCH

WITH NATURE IF WE CAN

CONSEQUENCES

JUST BECAUSE ADAM AND EVE DISOBEYED GOD
ALL OF MANKIND MUST LIVE AND DIE
CONSEQUENCES
MAN NOW SPEAKS DIFFERENT LANGUAGES FOR DISOBEYING
GOD WHEN THEY BUILT THE TOWER OF BABEL TOO HIGH
CONSEQUENCES
THE BIBLE SAYS LOVE YEA ONE ANOTHER
FOR YEA SHALL REAP WHAT YEA SHALL SOW
CONSEQUENCES

AN EYE FOR AN EYE A TOOTH FOR A TOOTH
THIS IS VERY IMPORTANT FOR YOU TO KNOW
CONSEQUENCES
PRESIDENT LINCOLN SAT IN THE BALCONY ANYWAY
AFTER BEING WARNED NOT
TO GO TO THE THEATER AND DIED

CONSEQUENCES
PRESIDENT NIXON WAS ALMOST IMPEACHED FROM OFFICE
FOR WATERGATE WHEN IT WAS DISCOVERED
THAT HE HAD LIED
CONSEQUENCES
WHEN WILL WE AS INTELLIGENT HUMAN BEING
BEGIN TO STOP AND THINK
THEN LISTEN AND LEARN
CONSEQUENCES
IF YOU CONTINUE TO PLAY AROUND WITH FIRE
EVENTUALLY YOU WILL GET BURNED

CONSEQUENCES

PROGRESS

NOT

PERFECTION

PERFECTION IS A PRODUCT OF THE WORLD'S FANTASY

PROGRESS IS THE STABLE CORE OF LIFE'S REALITY

IN VARIOUS PHASES OF LIFE YOU WORK TO GET IT RIGHT

EXPECTING RESULTS THAT WOULD MAKE

LIFE EASY AND BRIGHT

BUT YOU MUST BEWARE FOR PERFECTION ISN'T THERE

STEP BY STEP YOU MUST PROGRESS IF YOU DARE

WANTING PERFECTION IS OK TO RUN THROUGH YOUR MIND

BUT YOUR GOALS WILL BE REACHED

BY PROGRESSING THROUGH TIME

NOT REACHING PERFECTION COULD CAUSE YOU TO STOP

WHILE PROGRESSING STEP BY STEP YOU MAY TAKE A HOP

PROGRESS OVER PERFECTION YOU MUST CONTINUE TO TRY

LIFE WILL BE BETTER UNTIL THE DAY YOU DIE

EXCESS
BAGGAGE

SINNING IS THE FUEL THAT CAUSES GUILT TO GROW
GUILT WILL WEIGH YOU DOWN SPIRITUALLY
THIS YOU SHOULD KNOW
NOT HAVING A FREE SPIRIT YOU MAY FEEL
THAT YOU ARE LIVING IN JAIL
WORRYING ABOUT ALL THE NEGATIVITY IN LIFE
THINKING THIS MUST BE LIKE
LIVING IN HELL
NEGATIVITY CAN CAUSE LYING AND SOME OF US
LOOK UPON IT TO BE SMALL
BUT SOON THAT LITTLE LIE HATCHES OTHERS
THEY ARE HEAVY AND TALL
LIVING A LIFE THAT'S HONEST AND RIGHT
WILL HELP YOU TO ELIMINATE SIN
ELIMINATING SIN IS GOOD FOR THE SOUL
STOPPING THE GUILT FROM BUILDING UP WITHIN
IF THERE IS NOT GUILT HOLDING YOU DOWN
THERE IS NO REASON TO LIE
THEN YOU WILL ANSWER HONESTLY WHENEVER ANYONE
CONFRONTS YOU WITH THE QUESTION WHY
LYING SINNING AND GUILT ARE EXCESS BAGGAGE
YOU DON'T WANT
THEY WILL KEEP YOU SPIRITUALLY DOWN
BEING HONEST IN LIFE AND LOVING OTHERS WILL HELP
PREVENT YOU FROM
CARRYING EXCESS BAGGAGE AROUND

HE
WILL   BE
THERE

HOPING THAT YOUR CHILD GROWS UP AND BECOME

A LAWYER DOCTOR OR NURSE

OH HOW EVERY PARENT WISHES THIS TO HAPPEN AND PRAY

THAT THEY BECOME NOTHING WORSE

BUT AS A PARENT YOU MUST UNDERSTAND

THE FUTURE OF YOUR CHILD IS IN GOD'S HANDS

FROM THE TIME THEY WERE BORN TO THE TIME

THEY DIE GOD AS ALREADY PREPARED THE PLANS

AS A PARENT YOU MUST LET YOUR CHILD KNOW

ALL ABOUT THE GLORY OF GOD

SO WHEN THEY DO GO ASTRAY GETTING BACK TO GOD

FOR THEM WILL NOT BE HARD

YOU MUST REMEMBER WHEN TEMPTATION HAPPEN

TO HAVE COME YOUR WAY

THROUGH A LOT OF PRAYERS OF OTHERS

YOUR TROUBLES DIDN'T LAST OR STAY

SO PLEASE DON'T WORRY ABOUT GOD'S PLANS AND TRUST

IN THE POWER OF PRAYER

BECAUSE GOD WILL BE WITH YOU AND FOR YOUR

CHILD HE WILL BE THERE

MY STAR

THE NIGHT SKY IS GLEAMING WITH A SPLENDOR OF HOST

ALL EYES SHALL SEE THEM FROM EVERY POSITION

EVEN COAST TO COAST

AS I FOCUS ON A TRAIL SO BRIGHT THAT LOOKS

TO BE A GLASS SLIPPER

I MUST SUBMIT AND THEN RECOGNIZE THE FLAMBOYANCY

OF THE BIG DIPPER

OH WHAT A SIGHT IT WAS WHEN I DISCOVER THE ONE

THAT GLOWS RED

TO MY SURPRISE IT WASN'T A STAR BUT

THE PLANET MARS INSTEAD

FOR HOURS UPON HOURS I ENJOYED THIS

MAGNIFICENT HYPNOTIC STARE

AS MY MIND CONTINUED TO CALCULATE THE POSSIBILITY

OF LIFE OUT THERE

I SHALL BE PERSISTENT IN MY SEARCH OF THE HEAVENS

NO MATTER HOW FAR I KNOW

OUT OF THE MILLIONS OF THEM ONE OF THEM

MUST BE MY STAR

JUST

FINE

GOD HAS GIVEN ME A LIFE OF QUALITY

BUT UP UNTIL NOW I HAVE FAILED MY RESPONSIBILITY

THROUGH TEMPTATION I HAVE LOST A LOT OF TIME

DOING WHAT I WANT TO DO WITHOUT KEEPING GOD IN MIND

BUT NOW EVERY MORNING I KNEEL DOWN AND PRAY

THAT GOD FORGIVES THE PAST AND BLESSES ME TODAY

I TRY TO HELP SOMEONE WHENEVER I POSSIBLY CAN

FEELING THAT LIFE IS GOOD

WHEN FOLLOWING GOD'S COMMANDS

DOING ALL THAT I CAN IN HIS

HOLY NAME AND NOT ASKING WHY

RECEIVING HIS HEAVENLY BLESSING

UNTIL THE DAY I DIE

SO I SAY TO YOU JUST KEEP HIM IN MIND

FOR THE REST OF YOUR LIFE YOU WILL DO JUST FINE

POWER

THE TIME HAS COME FOR YOU TO KNOW

THERE'S A GREATER POWER THAT LOVES US SO

HE'S ALL AROUND CARING FOR YOU AND ME

BUT WITH OUR EYES HE'S HARD TO SEE

IF YOU LOOK DEEP INTO YOUR HEART

YOU WILL FIND HIM THERE

BRINGING PEACE JOY AND HAPPINESS TO ALL THAT CARE

JUST BELIEVE AND NEVER WORRY AGAIN

BECAUSE GOD GIVES YOU PEACE AND SERENITY WITHIN

HIGHER
POWER

WHO CAN WAKE EVERY MAN WOMAN BOY AND GIRL

NOBODY BUT MY HIGHER POWER

REMOVE ALL THE DRUGS FROM YOUR ADDICTIVE WORLD

NOBODY BUT MY HIGHER POWER

HE WILL LEAD YOU AND GUIDE YOU EVERYDAY

WHENEVER YOU ARE LOST HE WILL SHOW YOU THE WAY

WHATEVER THE PROBLEM HE'LL BE THERE ON TIME

ALL YOU HAVE TO DO IS CHOOSE TO KEEP HIM IN MIND

WHO CAN FORGIVE YOU OF ALL OF YOUR SINS

NOBODY BUT MY HIGHER POWER

REMOVE ALL THE GUILT BUILT UP WITHIN

NOBODY BUT MY HIGHER POWER

WHO CAN WIPE YOUR TEARS AND TROUBLES AWAY

NOBODY BUT MY HIGHER POWER

WHO CAN MAKE YOU FEEL GOOD AND PROUD TO SAY

NOBODY BUT MY HIGHER POWER

PRAISE
HIM

ALAS THE TIME HAS COME FOR ME TO SAY

I THANK THE LORD FOR HIS GLORY TODAY

HE MAKES ME WHOLE AND COMPLETE

MAKING ALL OF MY ENEMIES CRY IN DEFEAT

I WILL HONOR HIS NAME AND DO HIS WILL

BECAUSE JESUS CHRIST DIED AND MADE THE DEAL

NOW ALL I HAVE TO DO IS PRAY TO HIS HOLY NAME

THEN BE THANKFUL THAT LIFE FOR ME

WILL NEVER BE THE SAME

WHEN

I   AWAKE

THE DEVIL IS BUSY ALL THROUGH THE NIGHT

WAITING FOR A CHANCE TO SLIP INTO ME OUT OF SIGHT

TO PREVENT HIM FROM GETTING INTO MY HEAD

I FALL DOWN ON MY KNEES AS SOON AS I GET OUT OF BED

I PRAY TO GOD TO LEAD ME THROUGH THE DAY

THEN THE DEVIL WILL STEP BACK OUT OF MY WAY

SO I'M CAREFUL IN THE MORNING WHEN I AWAKE

MY SOUL THE DEVIL HAS NO CHANCE TO TAKE

I WOULD DO THIS ALSO IF I WERE YOU

FOR THE DEVIL IS WANTING YOUR SOUL TOO

GREATEST OF ALL

IF YOU THINK SEEING IS BELIEVING

BEWARE AND FOCUS TO PREVENT DECEIVING

WORK ON SURRENDERING YOUR WILL TO GOD

ALLOWING HIM TO PUT LOVE AND PEACE

INTO YOUR HEART

FOLLOWING SUGGESTIONS WILL HELP YOU

ALONG THE WAY

HUMBLING YOURSELF WILL WORK DAY BY DAY

THE GREATEST OF ALL IN HEAVEN IS A CHILD

SO HUMBLE YOURSELF LIKE ONE THEN

BE BLESSED ALL THE WHILE

MASTER
PLAN

WHEN YOUR PLANS DON'T WORK LIKE YOU

THINK THEY SHOULD

DON'T WORRY JUST PRAY

BECAUSE GOD'S PLANS ARE GOOD

I KNOW THAT HE WORKS IN MYSTERIOUS WAYS

HE CAN CHANGE THE CLOUDIEST INTO

A BRIGHT AND SUNNY DAY

TRUST IN HIM AND DO HIS HOLY WILL

WITH LOVE AND CARE

PEACE AND TRANQUILLITY HE WILL GIVE YOU TO SHARE

THERE'S A MASTER PLAN IN THIS WORLD

YOU MUST UNDERSTAND

WHAT HE HAS FOR YOU SHALL BE RECEIVED

FOLLOWING HIS COMMANDS

SO DON'T FORGET WHEN THINGS DON'T GO YOUR WAY

GOD COULD HAVE A BETTER PLAN FOR YOU TODAY

RAPTURE

THERE'S NO ONE PERFECT IN THIS WORLD TODAY

HE DIED ON THE CROSS BUT HE'S COMING

BACK THIS WAY

COMING FOR THE RIGHTEOUS AND THE PURE IN HEART

DESTROYING THE ANTICHRIST THE ONE WHO

EVEN FOOLED THE SMART

WE'LL BE CAUGHT UP IN THE SKY

DURING HIS HOLY CAPTURE

YOU MUST BE AWARE OF HIS BLESSED

PURIFYING RAPTURE

MY LORD JESUS CHRIST WILL

THEN CLAIM HIS THRONE

ALL THOSE WHO DIDN'T BELIEVE WILL BE DISOWNED

I PRAY THAT YOU HEAR WHAT I HAVE TO SAY

YOU MUST PREPARE FOR THE RAPTURE TODAY

LIFE
FOR   ME

THERE MUST BE A REASON FOR MY LIVING

MOST OF MY LIFE WONDERING WHY GOD IS SO GIVING

AM I HERE JUST TO SHUFFLE AND DEAL

OR BE FOR REAL AND DO HIS HOLY WILL

TROUBLES PROBLEMS AND TEMPTATION

ONLY CAUSE ME AGGRAVATION AND FRUSTRATION

CARING FOR OTHERS AND GIVING GOD MY TIME

LEADS TO HARMONY LOVE AND PEACE OF MIND

TODAY I WILL WORK CONSTANTLY

TO BECOME ONE WITH GOD

SO THAT MY TIME ON EARTH SHALL NOT BE HARD

MY
SOUL

YOU MUST TAKE A STAND AND MAKE A CHOICE
IN YOUR LIFE
TIME IS RUNNING OUT ALONE YOU CAN'T
WIN THE FIGHT
THERE'S A SPIRITUAL WAR BEING WAGED
IN THIS WORLD WE LIVE IN
NONE OF US WERE EVEN BORN AT THE TIME
THAT IT BEGAN
EACH OF US HAS A SPIRIT WE MUST CHOOSE
WHICH WAY IT GOES
AFTER LIFE IS OVER IN THIS WORLD THERE'S
ETERNITY YOU MUST KNOW
HEAVEN OR HELL THE LIFE WE LIVE DETERMINES
WHICH IT WILL BE
GETTING TO HEAVEN IS EASY AS COUNTING
ONE TWO THREE
GETTING TO HELL YOU MUST MAKE YOUR LIFE
AS DIFFICULT AS CAN BE
LOVING GOD WITH ALL YOUR HEART
MIND AND SOUL AND YOUR NEIGHBORS TOO
OR SUBMIT TO THE DEVIL'S DEADLY TEMPTATIONS
HE WILL PUT YOU THROUGH
THE RIGHT WAY OR THE WRONG WAY
FOR YOUR SOUL YOU HAVE A CHOICE TO MAKE
PRAY TO GOD FOR YOUR SOUL SO THE DEVIL
WON'T HAVE A CHANCE TO TAKE

**LONG
DISTANCE**

TALKING TO GOD IS DIFFICULT FOR SOME OF US TO DO

WAITING ON AN ANSWER NOT REALIZING

WHEN YOU HAVE GOTTEN THROUGH

JUST LIKE THE BIBLE DAYS OF OLD

HE COMMUNICATED THROUGH DREAMS

JACOB JOSEPH AND EZEKIEL ARE A FEW

WHO DIDN'T HAVE A PROBLEM IT SEEMS

THE BODY IS A TEMPLE THAT GOD HAS GIVEN US

TO DO HIS HOLY WILL

YOU MUST HAVE AN OPEN MIND PURE HEART AND

A CLEAN TEMPLE FOR THE DEAL

WITH ALL OF THESE IN PLACE PROPERLY

WHILE LOVING OTHERS IN TIME

GOD CAN COMMUNICATE WITH YOU

THROUGH YOUR DREAMS IN YOUR MIND

SHOW
AND
TELL

TO ALL OF YOU WHO THINK EASTER IS JUST A SHOW

THERE'S A VERY IMPORTANT STORY

THAT THE WORLD SHOULD KNOW

JESUS DIED ON THE CROSS TO SAVE US FROM OUR SINS

THAT THE DEVIL WITH HIS TEMPTATIONS

HAS BOUND SOME OF US IN

GOD KNEW THAT THE FLESH MADE

THE MIND AND THE SPIRIT OF HIS PEOPLE WEAK

SO HE SENT CHRIST TO TEACH US

HOW TO BE STRONG AND HOW TO BE MEEK

HE TAUGHT THE PEOPLE HOW TO PRAY

TO OUR FATHER UP ABOVE

ALSO TO DEFEAT THE DEVIL

BY RECEIVING AND SHARING GOD'S LOVE

EASTER IS A DAY THAT GOD SHOWS

THE KIND OF LOVE HE GIVES

LETTING HIS ONLY BEGOTTEN SON DIE

SO THAT WE MAY LIVE

IF ANY OF YOU THINK EASTER IS JUST

A SHOW FOR A DAY

THEN WE NEED TO SHOW LOVE

FOR EVERYONE EVERYDAY AND PRAY

STOP THE
VIOLENCE

IN GENESIS CAIN KILLED HIS BROTHER ABEL

THAT WAS THE BEGINNING

ONLY GOD IN HEAVEN KNOWS WHEN

THERE WILL BE AN ENDING

THROUGHOUT THE HISTORY OF MANKIND

MAN HAS CONTINUED TO KILL

WE NEED TO TURN FROM OUR WICKED WAYS

DOING ONLY GOD'S WILL

THE VIOLENCE WE HEAR ABOUT ON THE NEWS EVERYDAY

THE BIBLE TOLD US ALONE TIME AGO

IT WAS GOING TO BE THIS WAY

CHILDREN ARE KILLING EACH OTHER EVERYDAY

FOR NO REASON AT ALL

WE NEED TO PRAY BEFORE GOD DECIDES

IT'S TIME FOR GABRIEL'S CALL

WE NEED TO WORK TOGETHER TO GET

THE KILLING WITH GUNS SILENCED

FOR THE FUTURE OF OUR CHILDREN

SOMEHOW WE MUST STOP THE VIOLENCE

50

IN

VAIN

CLOSING MY MOUTH AND OPENING MY HEART

WILL GIVE ME THE WISDOM THAT I NEED TO START

LIVING A LIFE THAT I CAN BE PROUD OF

PRAYING TO MY FATHER IN HEAVEN UP ABOVE

DOING ALL THAT I CAN TO HELP OTHERS IS THE PLAN

KNOWING THIS IS ONE OF MY FATHER'S GREATEST COMMANDS

FOCUSING ON LIFE AND PUTTING DEATH WAY BEHIND

THINKING ONLY ABOUT THE POSITIVE WITH ALL OF MY TIME

WITH MY FATHER'S HELP MY LIFE WILL NEVER BE THE SAME

HOPEFULLY THEN MY LIVING SHALL NOT BE IN VAIN

OBEY

GOD TOLD ADAM AND EVE NOT TO EAT

FROM THE TREE OF LIVE

NOW ALL OF MANKIND MUST LIVE AND DIE

STRUGGLING THROUGH A LOT OF STRIFE

GOD TOLD PHARAOH TO LET MY PEOPLE GO

SO THEY CAN WORSHIP ME

DISOBEYING GOD CAUSED THE EGYPTIAN ARMY

TO BE KILLED BY DROWNING

IN THE SEA

SO WHY DO SOME OF US REFUSE

TO LISTEN TO THE WORDS OF GOD

ONLY TO SUFFER LIVING A LIFE

THAT TROUBLESOME AND HARD

DOING HIS WILL AND THANKING HIM

FOR GUIDING YOU ALONG THE WAY

IS ALL THAT HE ASK FOR YOU TO DO

SO HE CAN BLESS YOU EVERYDAY

READING THE BIBLE WILL HELP YOU

TO LEARN TO LIVE HIS WAY

TO LIVE A LIFE THAT PROSPEROUS

HIS COMMANDMENTS YOU MUST OBEY

DEEP
WITHIN

RISE UP AND WALK THE TIME HAS COME

YOU MUST UNDERSTAND

THE WORLD HAS WE KNOW IT IS PASSING AWAY

RECOGNIZE IT IF YOU CAN

LOOK AROUND YOU TO FEEL THE CHANGES

THAT ARE TAKING PLACE

REVELATION IS UPON US YOU MUST PREPARE

IF YOU DON'T IT WILL BE A DISGRACE

READ IT BELIEVE IT LIVE IT FOR THE FUTURE

WILL NOT WAIT

TRY YOUR BEST TO COMPREHEND THE MESSAGE

FOR YOUR SOUL YOU MUST RELATE

USE THE WISDOM AND KNOWLEDGE THAT HAS BEEN

PASSED ON TO YOU THROUGH TIME

I HAVE HEARD BY THE YEAR **2000**

DON'T BE CONFUSED IN **1999**

NO MAN KNOWS THE TIME THE DAY OR HOUR

IT WILL ALL BEGIN

IF YOU READ BELIEVE AND PRAY

YOU WILL FEEL IT DEEP WITHIN

ALREADY
A
WINNER

WHY BET OR PUT YOUR LIFE IN HUMAN HANDS

WHEN GOD HAS ALREADY PROVIDED FOR YOU

THE WORLD'S BEST INSURANCE PLAN

WHY SPEND YOUR MONEY AND TIME

TRYING TO WIN THE JACKPOT ALL YOUR LIFE

WHEN JESUS HAS ALREADY PAID THE PRICE SO WE

WOULDN'T HAVE TO GAMBLE ONLY TO WIN STRIFE

RIVER BOATS LAS VEGAS LOTTERIES HORSERACES

DOG RACES AND CASINOS WE SEARCH

WITH ALL THE MONEY AND TIME THAT WE SPEND

WHY NOT SPENT IT IN CHURCH

THE LORD IS MY SHEPHERD I SHALL NOT WANT

THAT IS WHAT THE BIBLE SAY

SO WHY DO WE PAY ATTENTION TO THE

DEVIL'S TEMPTATIONS TODAY

GOD WILL PROVIDE FOR ALL OF YOUR NEEDS

IF ONLY YOU RESIST TEMPTATION

NOT BECOMING A SINNER

FOR IF YOU BELIEVE AND TRUST IN GOD

THROUGH JESUS CHRIST YOU ARE

ALREADY A WINNER

DIVINE
INTERVENTION

THERE ARE ANGELS ALL AROUND US

IN THE SKY AND ON THE GROUND

ANGELICAL SPIRITS WORKING FOR GOD

TO HELP US IN NEED ESPECIALLY

WHEN THERE IS TROUBLE AROUND

THE BIBLE MENTION SO MANY ANGEL

THIS I DO PRAY TELL

LEADING AND HELPING MANY OF THE PEOPLE

IN THE OLD TESTAMENT YOU HEARD OF

GABRIEL MICHAEL AND RAPHAEL

HAS SOMETHING DRAMATIC EVER HAPPEN TO YOU

THEN YOU WONDER HOW YOU EVER SURVIVE

THEN YOU SAID TO YOURSELF OH HOW LUCKY I WAS

TO COME THAT CLOSE AND STILL BE ALIVE

SOMEONE SHOWS UP WHEN YOU REALLY NEEDED HELP

THEN GETS YOU GOING IN THE RIGHT WAY

THEN YOU SAY TO THEM OH WHAT A COINCIDENCE

THAT YOU HAPPENED TO SHOW UP TODAY

AS HUMANS IT IS HARD TO UNDERSTAND

GOD'S WISDOM BUT YOU MUST PAY STRICT ATTENTION

FOR I FEEL THERE IS NOT LUCK OR COINCIDENCE

ONLY GOD'S DIVINE INTERVENTION

HEAR YE

HEAR YE

INSTEAD OF BEING IN SCHOOL SOME KIDS
ARE OUT BUYING GYM SHOES OR RECORDS
EVEN GOING TO THE MOVIES AND SKIPPING CLASSES
IT IS PHENOMENAL HOW THE ATHLETES
RECORDING ARTISTS AND MOVIES STARS
HAVE THE POWER TO INFLUENCE THE MASSES
WITH ALL THIS POWER YOU WOULD THINK
THAT THEY COULD SEE THE LIGHT
USING THEIR INFLUENCE TO HELP OTHERS
TO UNDERSTAND LIFE BETTER BY GUIDING THEM RIGHT
BEFORE A GAME STARTS A TEAM WILL STOP
TO BOW THEIR HEADS THEN PRAY
A SINGER OR ACTOR WILL PRAY BEFORE
TAKING THE STAGE THAT GOD BLESSES THEM TODAY
MILLIONS OF PEOPLE ARE UNDER THE INFLUENCE OF
THE SUPER STARS SO MUCH POWER IN THEIR HANDS
SO WHY AREN'T THEY SAYING SOMETHING
POSITIVE OR ADVERTISE ABOUT GOD
AND HIS BLESSED PLANS
BEING BLESSED WITH WHAT THEY HAVE
MAKES IT EASY TO LET THE WORLD KNOW
THAT GOD SHOULD BE RECOGNIZE
FOR GOD GAVE THEM THE POWER
TO INFLUENCE THE MASSES HIS LOVE SHOULD
BE ADVERTISED

DEATH
DO   WE
PART

THE DEATH OF A LOVE ONE CAN BE DIFFICULT

FOR A PERSON TO OVERCOME

HAVING TO GO THROUGH LIFE WITHOUT THAT LOVE

IS VERY DEPRESSING FOR SOME

DOCTORS SAY IT COULD TAKE YEARS FOR

THE PAIN TO BE OVER

IT IS NOT SURPRISING FOR A PERSON TO START

HATING LIFE AND THEIR HEART TO GROW COLDER

THE REALITY OF DEATH MUST BE ACCEPTED BY ALL

IN ORDER TO LIVE ON

TALKING IT OVER WITH SOMEONE WILL HELP

YOU TO DEAL WITH BEING SCORNED

THERAPY WILL HELP YOU TO UNDERSTAND

YOU MUST CONTINUE TO LIVE LIFE

READING THE BIBLE CAN EASE YOUR HEART ACHE AND PAIN

GIVING YOU THE WILL TO FIGHT

ASHES TO ASHES DUST TO DUST LOSING A LOVE ONE

IS INEVITABLE AND HARD

LIFE GOES ON YOU MUST UNDERSTAND THAT IT IS IN

DEATH DO WE PART

LET   **GO**
     AND
LET   **GOD**

SURRENDERING MY WILL SEEMS HARD TO DO

BUT THAT IS THE ONLY WAY I WILL MAKE IT THROUGH

NOT DOING EVERYTHING MY WAY SEEMS INCONCEIVABLE

BUT TODAY MY HIGHER POWER CAN MAKE IT BELIEVABLE

I CAN'T HE CAN IS WHAT THEY SAY

THAT IS WHY I SURRENDER TO MY HIGHER POWER TODAY

ONE   DAY
AT
A   TIME

THERE ARE ONLY TWENTY FOUR HOURS IN A DAY

WHY DO WE AS ADDICTS THROW THEM AWAY

OUR HIGHER POWER GIVES US THIS TIME

TO BE HONEST WILLING AND OPEN MIND

WE SLAVE AT OUR JOBS EIGHT HOURS A DAY

SOME OF US SLEEP EIGHT HOURS AWAY

NOW THERE ARE EIGHT HOURS LEFT WHAT SHOULD WE DO

BE A SLAVE TO OUR ADDICTION OR GO

TO A MEETING AND MAKE IT THROUGH

THE CHOICE IS YOUR'S AND IT IS ALL UP TO YOU

BUT BEFORE YOU CHOOSE PUT THIS ON YOUR MIND

THE BEST WAY IS ONE DAY AT A TIME

STOP
AND
START

ARE YOU EVER TIRED OF TRYING TO KILL YOURSELF

RUSHING THROUGH LIFE BARELY ESCAPING DEATH

YOU SHOULD KNOW BY NOW YOU SHOULD MAKE A CHANGE

STOP USING DRUGS AND BECOME WILLING TO BE ORDAINED

YOUR HIGHER POWER HAS BE WAITING FOR YOU

SO HE CAN REMOLD AND REBUILD YOU TO START NEW

BELIEVING IN HIM AND TRUSTING IN HIS HOLY NAME

KNOWING THROUGH HIM THE DEVIL HAS NO CLAIM

YOUR ADDICTION WILL STOP THEN YOU CAN START GIVING

FEELING REBORN KNOWING YOU CAN START LIVING

```
            WHAT
TIME                 IS
          IT
```

WHAT TIME IS IT I NEED TO KNOW

ON A MISSION I KNOW I MUST GO

FEED MY ADDICTION NO I'VE BEEN THERE BEFORE

DEEP IN MY HEART THERE IS ANOTHER CORRIDOR

THROUGH TIME I FINALLY SEE THE LIGHT

THE TIME IS NOW TO STOP THE FIGHT

TO LIVE LIFE CLEAN HOW ABOUT YOU

THE TIME IS NOW WHAT ARE YOU GOING TO DO

UNITY

WHEN YOU ARE FEELING DOWN AND OUT

TALK TO SOMEONE WHO KNOWS WHAT IT ALL ABOUT

THE THERAPEUTIC VALUE OF ONE ADDICT HELPING

ANOTHER IS WITHOUT PARALLEL

SO GO SAT DOWN AND LISTEN TO THE STORY

THAT SOMEONE ELSE HAS TO TELL

WHEN YOU HAVE HEARD SOMETHING THAT YOU CAN

RELATE TO IN YOUR MIND

YOU SHOULD FEEL ASSURE THAT TOGETHER

THING WILL GET BETTER WITH TIME

DYING

HIGH

HUNDREDS OF ADDICTS ARE DYING EVERYDAY USING

SO I ASK MYSELF HOW CAN I STOP ABUSING

IN THE PROGRAM THEY ASK ME WHY

SO I TELL THEM I JUST DON'T WANT TO GET HIGH

BUT DEEP IN MY HEART THERE IS ANOTHER REASON

REALIZING WHEN USING I CAN DIE ANY SEASON

AFRAID OF THE TRUTH NOT WANTING TO FACE THE FACT

KNOWING TO THE STREETS I DON'T WANT TO GO BACK

NOW I TELL THE TRUTH WHEN THEY ASK ME WHY

I DON'T WANT TO BE ONE OF THEM DYING HIGH

```
                    CLEAN
          AND                 SOBER
```

WHY SHOULD I PICK UP TO DIE

KNOWING THAT USING ONLY CAUSES LOSING

HERE IN RECOVERY THERE IS A CHANCE FOR DISCOVERY

OF A BRAND NEW LIFE IF I WORK IT RIGHT

NOW I HAVE MADE UP MY MIND TO PUT IN THE TIME

TO LIVE LIFE SOBER SO THE PAIN WILL BE OVER

THANKING MY HIGHER POWER FOR EVERY BLESSED HOUR

HE HAS GIVEN ME TO BE HAPPY AND DRUG FREE

CHANGE

RUNNING FROM MY PROBLEMS HAS BEEN MY M.O.

BUT TODAY I RUN TO MEETING ITS BETTER I KNOW

TRYING TO AVOID REALITY LIKE I'VE DONE BEFORE

MAKES ME WONDER AND WORRY MORE AND MORE

BUT USING GOD TO BE MY GUIDE

WILL KEEP ME FROM DUCKING AND TRYING TO HIDE

SO TODAY I PRAY TO DO HIS WILL AND STAY STRONG

KNOWING WITH HIS HELP I CAN DO NO WRONG

BEGINNING

LIFE GETTING HIGH FOR ME IS OVER

KNOWING TO LIVE SOBER I MUST BE BOLDER

LETTING GO OF THE PAST HAS TOUCH MY SOUL

NOW THAT I'M MATURING AND GETTING OLD

BUT GOD STILL HAS A LOT FOR ME TO DO

I MUST OPEN MY MIND AND LET HIM THROUGH

WITH HIS POWER I MUST GO ON

RECOVERY FOR ME STARTS NOW THAT

THE DRUGS ARE GONE

```
               IT
WORK          SO          WORK
               IT
```

KEEPING YOUR PAST IN FRONT OF YOU

WILL HELP YOUR PRESENT DREAMS TO COME TRUE

REMEMBERING THE THINGS YOU DON'T WANT TO DO

WILL HELP YOUR RECOVERY GO SMOOTH FOR YOU

WORKING THE TWELVE STEPS ONE AT A TIME

ALONG WITH KEEPING GOD ON YOUR MIND

WILL PUT YOU ON THE STRAIGHT AND NARROW WAY

SO STAYING SOBER WILL BE EASY DAY BY DAY

THE WAY

SO YOU SAY THAT YOU WANT TO STAY CLEAN FOR LIFE

YOU ALSO WANT TO KNOW WHICH WAY IS RIGHT

GOING TO MEETING EVERY SINGLE DAY

TALKING TO YOUR SPONSOR WHEN YOU LOSE YOUR WAY

WILL GET YOU GOING ON THE RIGHT TRACK

TO STAY OFF DRUGS AND NEVER GO BACK

YOU ALSO NEED A POWER GREATER THAN YOUR OWN

PRAYING AND GOING TO CHURCH IS WHERE YOU BELONG

DOING THESE THINGS WILL GIVE YOU THE START

THEN GOD WILL WORK IN YOUR LIFE SO IT WON'T BE HARD

FAMILY
IN
RECOVERY

WE ARE A FAMILY TOGETHER THROUGH SHARING

LOOKING TO EACH OTHER FOR CONCERN AND CARING

POINTING OUT EACH OTHERS CHARACTER DEFECTS

LEARNING NOT TO RESPOND TO EACH OTHER WITH REFLEX

TAKING OUR TIME TO USE COGNITIVE THINKING

SO WE DON'T LEAVE HERE DRUGGING AND DRINKING

HELPING MY BROTHERS AND SISTERS SO THEY CAN SEE

THAT WE CAN CHANGE AND REMAIN A HAPPY FAMILY

SEARCHING

WHILE SEARCHING FOR AN ANSWER TO MY ADDICTION

I'VE LEARN TO BE OPEN MINDED AND FORGET

MY PREDICTIONS

FOLLOWING OTHER PEOPLE'S SUGGESTION ABOUT

THE WAY TO GO

GIVING UP ON THE PAST ABOUT THE THINGS I KNOW

LET GO AND LET GOD THEN STEP BACK OUT OF THE WAY

BELIEVE AND HAVE FAITH DAY BY DAY

TO MEETING ON A DAILY BASICS I MUST GO

LETTING OTHERS INTO MY LIFE ESPECIALLY

THE ONES THAT KNOW

ALL ABOUT SOBRIETY AND NOT GETTING HIGH

I WILL FEEL BETTER DAY BY DAY

UNTIL THE DAY I DIE

DON'T FORGET

HERE I AM FINALLY IN TREATMENT

AFTER ALL THE ABUSE AND YEARS OF RESENTMENT

WORKING ON MY PROGRAM AND DOING JUST FINE

SLEEPING GOOD AT NIGHT DOING THE DAY THREE MEAL I DINE

LOOKING BACK ON THE DAY BEFORE I CAME IN

I WAS BEATEN UP BROKEN DOWN AND STINKING OF GIN

BUT NOW I FEEL BETTER AFTER PUTTING IN SOME DAYS

MY BODY FEEL GOOD BUT MY MIND IS STILL CRAZED

THE DAY BEFORE I GOT HERE WAS A HELL OF A FIGHT

THIS I SHALL NEVER FORGET AND NEVER LOSE SIGHT

BECAUSE IF I GO OUT AND TRY TO GET HIGH

IT COULD BE THE ONE THAT CAUSES ME TO DIE

SLIPPING

INTO

DARKNESS

WHILE IN RECOVERY I WORK ON CHANGING MY THINKING

TRYING TO FORGET WHEN I WAS DRUGGING AND DRINKING

LEARNING TO COMMUNICATE WITH OTHERS COGNITIVELY

DISMISSING MY OLD HABITS AND WHO I USED TO BE

TAKING MY TIME TO GET CLOSER TO MY HIGHER POWER

FOCUSING ON MY SOBRIETY DAY BY DAY HOUR BY HOUR

BUT THERE ARE TIMES I MIGHT BEGIN TO FORGET

I'M SLIPPING INTO DARKNESS AND I IS WILL NOT SUBMIT

ONLY
ONE   FOR
ME

IF I EVER THINK THAT I COULD ONLY JUST HAVE ONE
I WOULD NEED TO THINK AGAIN BECAUSE IN MY CONDITION
I WOULD CRAVE TO HAVE SOME
ONCE I TRIED ONE PIECE OF CANDY A LONG TIME AGO
MY THIRTY-TWO TEETH ARE DOWN TO TEN
THIS YOU SHOULD KNOW
I DRANK ONE CAN OF BEER A COUPLE OF YEARS BACK
NOW ONE WON'T DO I NEED TWO OR THREE SIX-PACKS
THE WORD ADDICTION MEANS A WHOLE LOT TO ME
INSTEAD OF ONE CUP OF ICE CREAM
I WANT TO EAT ALL THAT I SEE
I THOUGHT I COULD DO JUST ONE HIT SIMPLY AS
DRINKING FROM A FOUNTAIN
AFTER TRYING TO DO JUST ONE I'M LOOKING AROUND
FOR THE MOUNTAIN
BEING ADDICTIVE TO EVERYTHING I TRY TO USE IN LIFE
I MUST BE CAREFUL BECAUSE TOO MUCH WILL
ONLY LEAD TO STRIFE
REMEMBERING I'M AN ADDICTIVE PERSON WILL HELP
ME TO LIVE
A LIFE THAT IS HONEST AND RIGHT UNTO MY ADDICTION
I WILL NOT GIVE
LIFE IS GOOD NOW THAT I'M AWARE OF MY ADDICTIVE PERSONALITY
KNOWING WHATEVER IT MIGHT BE IT WON'T BE
ONLY ONE FOR ME

QUEEN

SOME WOMEN OF THE WORLD ARE SOFT AND SMOOTH

AS A MOTHER PEARL

SOMETIME RAISING THEIR CHILDREN ALL ALONE

KNOWING THAT THE MAN

HAS LONG GONE FROM HOME BUT STILL SHE STRIVES

TO MAKE ENDS MEET

PRAYING TO GOD TO KEEP HER ON HER FEET

AFTER THE CHILDREN HAVE GROWN UP AND HAVE

SETTLED DOWN

SHE CAN BE PROUD TO SAY "**I VE EARN MY CROWN** "

SUNSHINE

EVERYTIME I SEE YOUR FACE

MY HEART SKIPS A BEAT

MY BLOOD PRESSURE BEGINS TO RISE

MY BODY GETS WEAK FROM HEAD TO FEET

LIKE SUNSHINE IN THE MORNING YOUR SMILE APPEARS

BRINGING JOY AND HAPPINESS FROM YOU TO ME

THAT MAKES ME GRIN FROM EAR TO EAR

YOU ARE THE ONE THAT MAKES

ME FEEL THIS WAY INSIDE

JUST KNOWING YOU FILLS ME

WITH HOPE JOY AND PRIDE

ONLY
YOU

WHENEVER I THINK OF A BEAUTIFUL FLOWER
BLOSSOMING IN THE MORNING DEW
IT REMINDS ME OF A PASSIONATE NIGHT AND MY MIND

WONDERS OFF TO YOU

MY BODY STARTS PULSATING LIKE A MACHINE

THEN I TELL MYSELF THIS IS ONLY A DREAM

THINKING OF THE PLEASANT TIMES

WE HAVE SPENT TOGETHER

MAKES ME HAPPY TO KNOW THAT OUR FRIENDSHIP

CAN LAST FOREVER

YOU ARE A VERY SPECIAL PERSON

IN MY LIFE TODAY

I'M BLESSED YOU CAME INTO MY LIFE

TO MAKE ME FEEL THIS WAY

YOU HAVE ALWAYS BEEN THERE

WHEN I HAVE NEEDED YOU

I KNOW OUR FRIENDSHIP WILL LAST FOREVER AND IT
WILL BE TRUE

STAR

ALAS ON THIS NIGHT I HAVE SEEN A STAR

OH SO BEAUTIFUL BRIGHT AND SHINING YOU ARE

YOU FILL MY WORLD WITH SO MUCH DELIGHT

ALL I CAN DO IS WISH UPON THIS STAR TONIGHT

WHEN YOU SPARKLE I LOSE ALL CONTROL

OH HOW I WISH I CAN TAKE YOU FOR A STROLL

BUT I KNOW THIS IS NOT POSSIBLE TO DO

SO I THANK THE HEAVENS THAT I HAVE MET YOU

WHEN YOU ARE GONE AWAY FROM ME TOO FAR

I WILL ENJOY MY PLEASANT

DREAMS OF A BEAUTIFUL STAR

BLACK
DIAMOND

THEY SAY DIAMONDS ARE A GIRL'S BEST FRIEND

BUT I KNOW A BLACK DIAMOND THAT WILL

MAKE YOUR HEAD SPIN

WHEN SHE WALKS TIME STOP TO TAKE A LOOK

WHEN IT COMES TO MAKING MEN HAPPY

SHE WROTE THE BOOK

HER BODY IS SHAPED AS FLAWLESS AS CAN BE

A BLIND MAN WILL GIVE HIS ARMS

FOR A CHANCE TO SEE

IMAGINE THE MOST BEAUTIFUL DIAMOND

YOU HAVE EVER SEEN

YOU WILL UNDERSTAND WHAT I MEAN

WHEN SHE WHERE A PAIR OF JEANS

IF YOU LOOK INTO HER

SEXY BEDROOM EYES

YOU WILL BE HYPNOTIZED AND BEGIN TO DREAM

ABOUT HER THIGHS

YOU COULD SPEND A LIFE TIME SEARCHING

ALL AROUND THE WORLD

JUST TO FIND SOMETHING AS FINE AS THIS

BLACK DIAMOND GIRL

SWEET

I KNOW A YOUNG LADY WHO'S OH SO SWEET

SHE'S ALWAYS QUIET AND DRESSES VERY NEAT

IF YOU NEEDED HELP SHE WOULD DO

THE VERY BEST SHE CAN

ALL SHE WANTS IS A CARING AND LOVING MAN

NEVER DISTURBING OTHERS AND LEAVING THEM ALONE

SOMETIMES WANTING TO BE BY HERSELF ON HER OWN

OH SO LOVING CARING AND KIND

SHE SHALL ALWAYS BE

THIS BEAUTIFUL LADY HAS ALWAYS BEEN SWEET TO ME

SUGAR

CANE

SWEET AS HONEY AS FINE AS A DIAMOND RING

WHENEVER I LOOK AT YOU ALL I WANT TO DO IS SING

SOFT AS COTTON SMOOTH AS AN OCEAN PEARL

ALL I WANT YOU TO DO IS ROCK MY WORLD

WHEN YOU WALK MY MIND STARTS TO SWIRL

I WOULD DO ANYTHING TO GET NEXT TO YOU GIRL

IF BY CHANCE I CAN GET TO KNOW YOU

MAYBE MY DREAMS WILL HAVE A CHANCE TO COME TRUE

WHEN WE GET TOGETHER MY LIFE

WILL NEVER BE THE SAME

THEN YOU WILL BE MY SWEET

FINE BROWN SUGAR CANE

VISION
OF
LOVELINESS

NIGHT AFTER NIGHT I DREAM OF A VISION OF
ENCHANTING LOVELINESS
DAY AFTER DAY I SEARCH FOR THIS BEAUTY
THROUGHOUT MY LIFE I HAVE MISSED
MY HEART POUNDS WITH ANTICIPATION OF LOVE
I CANNOT FORGET
AWAITING THE TASTE OF HER BODY
TO HER TENDER KISS I WILL SUBMIT
LIPS THAT ARE OF PERFECTION
TO NO END THEY SOOTHE
ALAS MY SEARCH IS OVER
THE SUN HAS SHINED ON ME
FOR ON THIS DAY IN HISTORY
THE BEAUTY OF MY DREAMS I SEE
STANDING THERE LIKE A GODDESS
OH WHAT A VOLUPTUOUS VIEW
THIS VISION OF LOVELINESS IN MY DREAMS
I KNOW NOW IS YOU

MAGNIFICENT

GARDEN

ONLY FLOWERS CAN COMPARE

TO THE ROSIENESS OF YOUR CHEEKS

THE AROMA OF YOUR LILAC HAIR

MAKES ME OH SO WEAK

THE SCENTS OF PETUNIAS ENGULF

ME WITH YOUR TEMPTATION

YOU FILL ME WITH SO MUCH DELIGHT

WITH THE TASTE OF YOUR CARNATION

I'M FILLED WITH PASSION FOR YOUR TULIPS

OH WHAT A SIGHT TO BEHOLD

IT'S HEAVENLY TO BE NEAR YOUR DAFFODIL

WHEN YOUR PETALS BEGIN TO UNFOLD

OH WHAT A PRECIOUS HONOR IT IS

TO BE ONE OUT OF ALL THE MEN

TO HAVE THE OPPORTUNITY TO EXPERIENCE

THIS MOMENT IN YOUR MAGNIFICENT GARDEN

WITHOUT
YOU

OH_____ SINCE I'VE BEEN AWAY FROM YOU

IT'S HARD TO EXPRESS THE TORMENT

I'M GOING THROUGH

JUST THE THOUGHT OF YOU NOT SHARING MY LIFE

MAKES MY HEART ACHE BUT I WON'T

GIVE UP THE FIGHT

THE LOVE I HAVE FOR YOU MEANS

MORE TO ME THAN LIVING

THERE MUST BE A WAY SOMEHOW THAT YOU

CAN START BELIEVING

JUST LIKE THE STARS IN THE NIGHT SKY

COMPLIMENT THE MOON

I WOULD BE NOTHING WITHOUT YOU IN MY LIFE SOON

JUST LIKE THE RAIN CAUSES THE FLOWERS TO GROW

I NEED YOUR LOVE IN MY LIFE TO MAKE ME GO

I PROMISE THAT I WILL LOVE YOU FOREVER AND THAT

IT WILL BE TRUE

SO PLEASE RE-LIGHT THE FIRE

BECAUSE I CAN'T LIVE WITHOUT YOU

ONE
HUNDRED PERCENT

THERE ARE WOMEN IN THIS WORLD TODAY

WHO REALLY NEED TO FALL ON

THEIR KNEES AND PRAY

RUNNING IN THE STREETS

FROM MAN TO MAN ALL WILD

NOT HAVE ANY RESPECT EVEN

NEGLECTING THEIR CHILD

BUT YOU ARE A WOMAN NO LESS THAN

ONE HUNDRED PERCENT

BEAUTIFUL AS THE QUEEN OF EGYPT

SITTING ON THE NILE

ALL THE TIME HAVING SUCH A GRACIOUS SMILE

TAKING YOUR TIME TO TEACH YOUR CHILDREN

HOW TO RESPECT

HELPING WITH THEIR HOMEWORK

MAKING SURE IT'S CORRECT

LOVING YOUR MAN WITH ALL OF YOUR HEART FOREVER

TAKING CARE OF HIS NEEDS BEING VERY CLEVER

MORE WOMEN NEED TO PAY ATTENTION TO YOU JUST

TO GET A HINT

BECAUSE YOU ARE A REAL SPECIAL WOMAN

ONE HUNDRED PERCENT

BABY
BLUES

HOW CAN YOU LOOK AND NOT BECOME CONFUSED

IF BY CHANCE YOU HAPPEN TO LOOK

INTO THOSE BABY BLUES

OH SO SOFT SWEET AND INNOCENT THEY ARE

THE MOST BEAUTIFUL SET OF EYES I'VE SEEN BY FAR

LOOKING DEEP INTO THEM MAY CAUSE

YOU TO BECOME HYPNOTIZED

FOR A MOMENT YOUR HEART MAY STOP

THEN YOU ARE ENERGIZED

I'M GLAD I'VE HAD THE CHANCE TO HAVE MET YOU

A SWEET AND KIND PERSON WITH THE BABY BLUES

SPECIAL

SHE CAME INTO MY LIFE OUT OF NOWHERE

WHATEVER THE PROBLEM SHE TRIES TO CARE

WHENEVER SHE GREETS YOU IT'S ALWAYS WITH A SMILE

READY AND WILLING TO EVEN PLAY WITH A CHILD

SWEET AS A HONEYCOMB THAT THE BEES GATHER AROUND

IN ALL MY WORLDLY TRAVELS A KINDER PERSON

AS YET TO BE FOUND

A PERSON LIKE HER I THOUGHT COULD ONLY

EXIST WITHIN MY MIND

BUT NOW I KNOW I'M NOT DREAMING

SHE IS REAL THIS TIME

NO MATTER WHAT I HAVE TO DO

I MUST LET HER KNOW

THAT I DO NOTICE HER AND REALLY

APPRECIATE HER SO

THE TIME WE SPENT TOGETHER

MAKES ME FEEL OH SO GOOD

IF BY CHANCE SO SPECIAL TIME

I WANT TO SPEND IF I COULD

MY

DEAR

I'M AMONG THE ELITE EVERY TIME YOU

GRACE ME WITH YOUR PRESENCE

YOU SOOTHE MY SOUL WITH YOUR SMILE

I MUST SUBMIT TO THE ESSENCE

YOUR STUNNING EYES PENETRATE

I'M WEAK FOR YOUR ROMANCE

THE DAZZLING AFFECT OF YOUR AROMA

HAS MY HEAD SWIRLING I'M STUMBLING IN A TRANCE

I SURRENDER ALL THAT I AM AND I

ACKNOWLEDGE WITH A TEAR

THERE IS NO ONE IN THIS WORLD THAT COMPARES

TO YOU MY DEAR

SOUL
MATE

BEYOND THE NORMAL REALM OF RELATIONSHIPS
THERE IS A BOND KNOWN TO FEW

AS SOUL MATES

THIS HEAVENLY UNION COMMISSIONED BY GOD IS COMMON

ONLY TO THE TWO SPIRITS THAT RELATE

HAVING MET A TOTAL STRANGER

THEN LOOKING DEEP INTO THEIR EYES

THEN FEELING A CHILLING FIRE

DOWN TO THE BONE

THE FEELING OF SERENITY AND COMFORT

ENGULF YOUR BODY AND MIND TO A POINT

YOU HAVE NEVER KNOWN

THE CHANCE COULD BE A MILLION TO ONE

FOR SOME TO EXPERIENCE THIS UNIQUE

COSMIC EMBRACE

BUT BEING FORTUNATE PERHAPS TO BE THAT ONE

YOU SHALL NEVER FORGET THAT

EUPHORIC TASTE

WITH ALL THE LOVE THAT I CAN ACQUIRE

THEN SEAL WITH A KISS I WILL TAKE

THEN RETAIN IT WITHIN MY HEART

FOR ONLY YOU MY SOUL MATE

VICTORIA
SECRETS

THERE'S A HEAVENLY BODY I'VE BEEN BLESSED

TO BEHOLD THIS NIGHT

MORE BEAUTIFUL THEN HALEY'S COMET

BRIGHTER THAN ANY STAR IN SIGHT

CAPTURING A GLIMPSE WILL MAKE ME WANT

TO SEE MORE AND MORE

THERE MUST BE A WAY FOR ME TO EXCESS

THE MAGNIFICENT CORRIDOR

OUT OF ALL THE STAR IN OUR GALAXY

UPON WHICH I MAY FOCUS ON TO GAZE

FOCUSING ON THIS HEAVENLY BODY CAUSES MY HEAD

TO SPIN INTO A CRAZY DAZE

THERE MUST BE A WAY I CAN CAPTURE

THIS ENCHANTING BEING

INTO MY STARRY EYED SCOPE

THEN KEEP IT THERE UNTIL THE END OF TIME

TO GIVE ME PLEASURE THIS I WILL HOPE

LOSING SIGHT OF THE PLEASURE THAT I RECEIVE

WILL FILL MY HEART WITH REGRETS

FORCING ME TO RELINQUISH MY PRECIOUS QUEST

FOR VICTORIA SECRETS

YOU
BETTER
RECOGNIZE

BEHOLD THE MOST BEAUTIFUL AND THE MOST

POWERFUL FORCE IN THE UNIVERSE

MORE POWERFUL THAN A NUCLEAR BOMB

THROUGHOUT THE HISTORY OF MANKIND

THIS POWER IS KNOWN AS THE LOVE OF MOM

FROM THE TIME OF BIRTH A CHILD KNOWS OF

NO OTHER FORCE AROUND

AS AN ADULT THEY WILL RECOGNIZE THIS POWER

ESPECIALLY WHEN THEY ARE FEELING DOWN

MOTHERS ARE SO IMPORTANT TO THE CONTINUING

EXISTENCE OF ALL MANKIND

WITHOUT THE PREDOMINANT FORCE OF A MOTHERS LOVE

A PERSON COULD LOSE THEIR MIND

SO I THANK GOD FOR ALL MOTHERS NO MATTER

WHAT COLOR SHAPE OR SIZE

TO ALL THE PEOPLE IN THE WORLD

YOU MUST KNOW THIS IS A FORCE

YOU BETTER RECOGNIZE

TEACHER'S
PET

WITH ALL THE ATTENTION YOU HAVE FOCUSED

OH SO CARINGLY MY WAY

MAKES ME THINK ABOUT YOU WITH ANTICIPATION

ABOUT THE THINGS WE WILL DO TODAY

YOU MAKE ME FEEL SPECIAL WHEN YOU QUESTION ME

WITH OTHER STUDENTS AROUND

SO MANY DAYS YOU HAVE LIFTED MY SPIRITS

REMOVING MY FROWN

IT'S DIFFICULT FOR ME TO EXPRESS

THE WAY I REALLY DO FEEL

BUT I CAN SAY FOR A TEACHER YOU ARE

ONE OF THE BEST WITH CONCERNS OH SO REAL

IT'S GOOD TO HAVE A TEACHER AROUND WHO UNDERSTAND

THE WAY MY MIND OPERATES

MAKING EXPRESSING MYSELF AND COMMUNICATING

WITH YOU OH SO EASY TO RELATE

I KNOW THAT YOU BELIEVE THAT HANDS ON EXPERIENCE

IS THE BEST TEACHER AND I AGREE WITH THAT

THE MORE I LEARN FROM YOU MAKES ME WANT

TO BECOME THE TEACHER'S PET

SAPPHIRE

SLEEK SLENDER AS GRACEFUL AS A GAZELLE

ENVISIONING YOUR BEAUTY WILL CAUSE THINGS TO SWELL

EYES SO SOFT AND AS GLAMOROUS AS CAN BE

I WOULD GIVE ALL THAT I OWN JUST TO BE WITH THEE

YOU MELT MY HEART WITH ALL THAT I DESIRE

WHEN I'M NEXT TO YOU THE DEPTH OF MY SOUL IS ON FIRE

IF BY CHANCE YOU CAN FEEL THE SAME WAY OR HIGHER

THEN MY LOVE WILL FLOURISH WITH YOU

MY SPARKLING SAPPHIRE

GIVING
LOVE

THE TYPE OF LOVE THAT I WANT TO GIVE TO YOU

YOUR HEART OR MIND CANNOT BELIEVE OR CONCEIVE

IT TO BE TRUE

I WANT TO GIVE YOU THE LOVE THAT YOU HAVE ALWAYS

DREAMED OF

THAT SPECIAL KIND OF LOVE THAT ONLY COMES

FROM UP ABOVE

MY BODY AND MIND LONES FOR THE TENDERNESS

OF YOUR REALITY

ALL I NEED IS FOR YOU TO LOVE AND BELIEVE IN ME

I HAVE WAITED OH SO VERY LONG FOR THE THRILL

OF YOUR TENDER TOUCH

BECAUSE HAVING THE LOVE THAT YOU POSSESS

MEANS OH SO VERY MUCH

YOUR REALITY IS MY DESTINY

AS LONG AS I SHALL LIVE

TO HAVE YOU WITHIN MY HEART

ALL MY LOVE I SHALL GIVE

BEAUTY
BEYOND
COMPARE

WOMEN SPEND MILLIONS OF DOLLARS EVERY YEAR

TRYING TO MAKE THEMSELVES BEAUTIFUL

TRYING THEIR BEST TO WIN A MAN

BEING OH SO SWEET AND LOVEABLE

NAILPOLISH HAIRDOS EYELASHES

CONTACT LENSES AND WIGS THEY BUY TO WEAR

EXERCISING DIETING AND BODY SHAPING

ALL THE TIME WANTING SOME MAN TO CARE

BUT YOU HAVE NOTHING TO FEAR OR WORRY ABOUT

THE CONTEST HAS BEEN WON BY YOU

WITH ALL THE BEAUTY THAT YOU POSSESS

ALL THE WOMEN IN THE WORLD ARE THROUGH

WITH EYES THAT SPARKLE LIKE DIAMONDS

A SMILE THAT CAN STOP THE RAIN

A BODY THAT CAN CAUSE AN ACCIDENT

WHILE DRIVING ALL MEN INSANE

AS WEAK AS I AM FOR YOUR LOVE

I SURRENDER AND I MUST DECLARE

YOU ARE THE MOST MAGNIFICENT WOMAN

I HAVE EVER SEEN

WITH BEAUTY BEYOND COMPARE

MY
DARLING
DEAR

ONCE AGAIN THIS SPECIAL DAY HAS COME

IN YOUR LIFE MY DEAR

ALL I CAN DO IS THINK ABOUT THAT PRECIOUS CHILD

I HELD SO NEAR

THROUGH THE YEARS ON THIS DAY

I THOUGHT OF NO OTHER BUT YOU

I'VE ALWAYS WANTED FOR YOU TO KNOW

THAT I CARED AND MY LOVE IS TRUE

I KNOW IT'S HARD TO FORGET THE PAST

BUT I PRAY THAT YOU FORGIVE

BY ACCEPTING MY LOVE AND MY TEARS

FOR THE TYPE OF LIFE I LIVE

WITH ALL MY HEART AND THE LOVE A MOTHER HAS

SOMETIMES WITH A TEAR

I WANT THIS DAY TO BE SPECIAL FOR YOU

HAVE A HAPPY BIRTHDAY MY DARLING DEAR

CAPTURE
THE
GOLD

MARRIAGE IS A SACRED UNION

BETWEEN A WOMAN AND A MAN BLESSED BY GOD

FOR BETTER OR WORSE RICHER OR POORER

IN SICKNESS OR HEALTH

UNTIL DEATH DO THEY PART

GOLD IS A PRECIOUS METAL IN CERTAIN FORMS

IT IS CONSIDERED TO BE

A PRICELESS POSSESSION

THE COMBINATION OF BOTH OF THESE

WILL CREATE THE SETTING FOR

A VERY SPECIAL OCCASION

IT TAKES LOVE TRUST HONESTY AND PATIENCE

TO ENDURE FOR SUCH A LONG TIME

THROUGH UPS AND DOWNS CHILDREN GRANDCHILDREN

EVEN GREAT GRANDCHILDREN

WITHOUT LOSING YOUR MIND

CONGRATULATION TO YOU ON YOUR

GOLDEN WEDDING ANNIVERSARY DAY

MAY YOUR LOVE NEVER GROW OLD

FOR THE LOVE YOU HAVE SHARED WAS STRONG ENOUGH

FOR THE TWO OF YOU TO CAPTURE THE GOLD

UNDERSTANDING

THERE WERE TIMES IT SEEMS THAT WE COULDN'T GET
AN UNDERSTANDING BETWEEN EACH OTHER
SOMETIMES I EVEN ASK MYSELF DO YOU REALLY CARE
FOR ME OR MY MOTHER
BUT AS TIME PAST ON I SLOWLY BEGAN TO SEE
YOUR WISDOM AND CAME TO UNDERSTAND
THE TYPE OF LOVE THAT YOU WERE GIVING ME
WAS THE KIND I NEEDED TO BECOME A MAN
THROUGH GOOD TIMES AND BAD YOU WERE THERE
WHENEVER I NEEDED YOU
TO SHOW ME THE RIGHT THINGS
THAT A RESPONSIBLE MAN SUPPOSED TO DO
EVERY NIGHT I PRAY TO GOD TO KEEP
YOU HEALTHY AND STRONG
SO THAT THE LIFE THAT YOU ARE LIVING
WILL BE PROSPEROUS AND LONG
I THANK GOD FOR HAVING A FATHER THAT TOOK
THE TIME TO SHOW ME THE RIGHT WAY
I JUST WANT TO SAY THAT I LOVE YOU AND I PRAY
THAT YOU HAVE A
BLESSED AND HAPPY FATHER'S DAY

GUARDIAN
ANGEL

WHEN MY WORLD SEEMS THE CLOUDIEST YOU BRING ME

NOTHING BUT SUNSHINE

WHENEVER I'M IN TROUBLE AND EVERYONE ELSE

HAS LEFT MY SIDE

YOU ARE ALWAYS THERE ON TIME

I BELIEVE THAT GOD MUST HAVE KNOWN

LONG BEFORE I WAS BORN

THAT I NEED SOMEONE IN MY LIFE

WHO I COULD REALLY DEPEND ON

I JUST WANT TO THANK YOU FOR ALL

THE LOVE YOU DIRECTED MY WAY

I JUST WANT TO SAY I'LL LOVE YOU FOREVER

MAY GOD BLESS YOU WITH

A HAPPY AND PRECIOUS MOTHERS DAY

GRANNY

SOMETIMES I FEEL SAD WHEN MOM AND DAD

ARE NOT AROUND

I PICK UP THE PHONE AND CALL THE MOST

LOVING PERSON I KNOW TO BE FOUND

YOU MAKE ME FEEL BETTER JUST TALKING

TO YOU ANYTIME

YOU ARE THE SWEETEST PERSON I COULD EVER

HAVE ON MY MIND

YOU LISTEN TO WHATEVER MY PROBLEMS MIGHT BE

USING WISDOM AND GOOD JUDGMENT EXPLAINING

EVERYTHING CLEAR TO ME

I JUST WANT TO SAY I'LL LOVE YOU FOREVER AND IT

SHOULD BE A LAW THAT EVERYONE IN THE WORLD

SHOULD HAVE SOMEONE TO LOVE THEM

LIKE MY DEAR SWEET GRANDMA

FOR

YOU

THIS DAY HAS BEEN SAT ASIDE TO HONOR NO OTHER

NO ONE EXCEPT FOR YOU MY DEAR SWEET MOTHER

THE LOVE YOU GAVE ME WILL LAST FOR ALL TIME

YOU SHOULD KNOW THAT I LOVE YOU WITH

ALL MY HEART AND MIND

IF ONLY I COULD REACH INTO THE HEAVENS

NO MATTER HOW FAR

JUST TO CAPTURE AND GIVE

TO YOU A BRIGHT AND SHINING STAR

I WILL DO ANYTHING FOR YOU THEN BE PROUD TO SAY

I OWE MY LIFE TO YOU AND I WISH YOU

A VERY HAPPY MOTHER'S DAY

HEAVEN BOUND

FROM THE TIME THAT YOU WERE BORN YOU KNEW

THIS DAY WOULD COME

DON'T FEEL SAD YOU DID YOUR BEST AND ALWAYS

HELPED SOMEONE

YOU RAISED YOUR CHILDREN TO BE THE VERY BEST

THAT THEY COULD BE

TAKE PRIDE IN YOURSELF THEY ARE INDEPENDENT

YOU WERE THERE TO SEE

IT WAS A HARD FOUGHT BATTLE GOING THROUGH LIFE

BUT YOU PREVAILED WITH THE HELP OF GOD AND WON

THE FIGHT

SO NOW THE TIME HAS COME TO GREET GOD

WITH A SMILE DON'T FROWN

BECAUSE YOU WILL SEE HIM FOR YOUR SOUL IS

HEAVEN BOUND

NEVER

BE   **THE**

SAME

YOU HAVE OUR DEEPEST SYMPATHY ON

THE BEHALF OF GOD

WE KNOW THE LOSS OF YOUR LOVE ONE

WILL BE TAKING VERY HARD

YOU MUST REMEMBER IN YOUR TIME OF GRIEF

YOU ARE NOT ALONE

BECAUSE GOD WILL COMFORT YOU WHEN HE CALLS

YOUR LOVED ONE HOME

JUST PRAY TO HIM AND READ THE BIBLE

TO EASE THE PAIN

BECAUSE HE KNOWS LIFE FOR YOU WILL

NEVER BE THE SAME

SPEEDY
RECOVERY

I'M SORRY THAT YOU ARE IN THE HOSPITAL

FEELING A LITTLE ILL

ARE THOSE NURSES MAKING YOU TAKE

THOSE FUNNY COLOR PILLS

DON'T WORRY BE PATIENT THOSE DOCTORS

ARE THE BEST

HEAVEN KNOWS YOU WILL BE ALL RIGHT

AFTER A LITTLE REST

IF YOU CAN WATCH SO TELEVISION IT WILL HELP

PAST AWAY THE TIME

SOON YOU WILL BE BACK AT HOME

FEELING JUST FINE

IF YOU NEED TO TALK TO SOMEONE

YOU CAN ALWAYS CALL ME

I SINCERELY WISH YOU A VERY

HAPPY AND SPEEDY RECOVERY

**HOME
TO
STAY**

HOW ARE YOU IT'S SUCH A LOVELY DAY

HERE ARE A FEW WORDS A WOULD LIKE TO SAY

YOU WILL BE FEELING GOOD IN ALMOST NO TIME

GOD HAS THE POWER TO HEAL YOUR BODY AND MIND

JUST PRAY TO HIM AND HAVE FAITH IN HIM EVERYDAY

SOON YOU WILL BE FEELING GOOD COMING

HOME WITH ME TO STAY

GETTING

BETTER

I KNOW YOU ARE NOT FEELING GOOD TODAY

TRY TO SMILE AND PRAY GOD WILL MAKE IT OK

SOMETIMES ILLNESS IS PART OF THE MASTER'S PLAN

SO DON'T WORRY I KNOW THAT GOD WILL

DO ALL THAT HE CAN

SOON YOUR TROUBLES WILL BE OVER

YOU WILL BE BACK ON YOUR FEET

FEELING STRONGER AND HAPPIER

SMILING AT EVERYONE YOU MEET

HE CAN

JESUS HEALED THE SICK

THEN RAISED THE DEAD

JUST HAVE FAITH AND BELIEVE

IN YOUR HEART WHAT HE SAID

YOU WILL FEEL BETTER KNOWING

THAT YOU ARE NEVER ALONE

THEN THANK GOD BECAUSE SOON

YOU WILL BE ON YOUR WAY HOME

OOPS

ACCIDENTS HAPPEN I'M SORRY IT WAS YOU

AFTER SOME TIME IN A CAST IT WILL

FEEL LIKE NEW

THINK ABOUT ALL THE FINE PEOPLE

YOU WILL GET TO MEET

WHAT A CONVERSATION PIECE I REALLY DO THINK

IT WILL BE NEAT

SO KEEP YOUR CHIN UP AND DON'T LET

IT GET YOU DOWN

BECAUSE ACCIDENTS CAN HAPPEN

TO ANYONE IN TOWN

BELOVED

I KNOW YOU WILL BE FINE SO PLEASE DON'T WORRY

IF YOU GET BORED OPEN

THE BIBLE AND READ A GOOD STORY

THE LOVE WE HAVE FOR EACH OTHER

WILL GET US THROUGH THIS

I'LL BE THERE SOON TO SEE YOU

SO SAVE ME A KISS

WHEN YOU GET BETTER YOU WILL BE COMING ON HOME

THEN MY BELOVED WILL BE BACK AT THE THRONE

NO PAIN
NO GAIN

RIGHT NOW YOU MAY NOT FEEL

IT'S WORTH ALL THE PAIN

BUT ONCE YOU SEE THAT SMILING FACE

YOU WILL NEVER FEEL THE SAME

HOLDING YOUR CHILD SO CLOSE

NEAR AND DEAR TO YOUR HEART

YOU WILL FORGET ALL ABOUT THE PAIN

NEVER WANTING THE TWO OF YOU TO PART

SO WHEN THE PAIN HITS

IT'S OK TO SCREAM OUT LOUD

BECAUSE SOON YOU WILL BE A PROUD MOTHER

HOLDING YOUR CHILD

CHANGING

TIMES

THERE ARE TIMES YOU ARE UP

THEN TIMES YOU ARE DOWN

BUT PLEASE DON'T LET THIS

CAUSE YOU TO WEAR A FROWN

THINK OF THE GOOD TIMES

BEFORE YOUR PRESENT CONDITION

THEN CLEAR YOUR MIND OF ALL

NEGATIVE PREDICTION

THINGS WILL GET BETTER YOU MUST

BELIEVE THIS TO BE TRUE

IN NO TIME WE WILL BE TOGETHER

JUST LIKE WE USED TOO

SECOND
CHANCE

I'M SORRY THAT YOU ARE LYING

IN THAT HOSPITAL BED

CHEER UP AND THANK GOD

YOU COULD HAVE LOSE YOUR HEAD

RECOVERY WILL TAKE

A LITTLE MORE THAN NORMAL TIME

JUST THINK POSITIVE AND KEEP

GOD ON YOUR MIND

IN TIME YOU WILL BE

STRONG AND READY TO ROLL

SO PRAY AND THANK GOD FOR A SECOND CHANCE

TO LIVE TO BE OLD

SMILE

PLEASE TRY YOUR BEST TO KEEP

A SMILE ON YOUR FACE

EVEN THOUGH IT'S NOT EASY FOR YOU

TO BE IN THAT PLACE

THE PROBLEM YOU HAVE WILL HEAL IN TIME

FEELING BETTER YOU MUST KNOW

STARTS IN THE MIND

SOON YOU WILL BE SMILING

FEEL GOOD FULL OF ENERGY YOU KNOW

JUMPING TO YOUR FEET WHEN THE DOCTOR

SAYS IT'S TIME YOU CAN GO

FEELING
GOOD

I'M SORRY THAT YOU ARE IN THE HOSPITAL

THE WAY YOU FEEL WON'T LAST FOREVER

I'LL BET A MILLION TO ONE VERY SOON

YOU WILL BE FEELING BETTER

THE DOCTORS AND NURSES SAID

THEY HAVE NEVER SEEN ANYONE LIKE YOU

I KNOW YOU ARE DRIVING THEM UP A WALL

WITH THE THINGS THAT YOU DO

AS YOU GET BETTER THEY WILL TELL YOU

THAT YOU WILL BE LEAVING IN DUE TIME

BEFORE YOU LEAVE DO ME A FAVOR AND ASK THEM

TO CHECK OUT YOUR MIND

BALL

BEING IN THE HOSPITAL FOR A COUPLE OF DAYS IN BED

WILL GIVE THE DOCTORS A CHANCE TO CHECK

THAT THUMPING IN YOUR HEAD

YOU SHOULD BE ALL RIGHT AND FEEL JUST FINE

SOME REST SHOULD RELIEVE

ALL THE TENSION ON YOUR MIND

WHEN YOU ARE READY JUST GIVE ME A CALL

THEN WE CAN TALK ABOUT THE NIGHT BEFORE

WHEN YOU PARTIED AND HAD A BALL

WHERE
YOU
BELONG

THE HOSPITAL IS THE BEST PLACE FOR YOU TO BE

I KNOW THAT YOU WANT TO BE AT HOME WITH ME

THE DOCTORS SAID YOU NEED TO TAKE ANOTHER TEST

SURELY BEING THERE YOU WILL GET

THE RIGHT AMOUNT OF REST

ONCE THE DOCTORS ARE FINISHED AND YOU ARE

FEELING LIKE NEW I WILL COME TO SEE YOU

WE WILL SPEND TIME DOING WHATEVER YOU WANT TO DO

WHEN THE TIME COMES AND THEY SAY YOU CAN GO HOME

I WILL BE THE HAPPIEST PERSON IN TOWN

TO HAVE YOU BACK WHERE YOU BELONG

DREAM
ABOUT
ME

RIGHT NOW MY HEART POURS OUT TO YOU

THE LOVE WE HAVE I KNOW WILL GET US THROUGH

WHEN I WAS IN THE HOSPITAL YOU CAME TO SEE ME

SO EVERY NIGHT WHEN I GO TO SLEEP

I WILL DREAM OF THEE

I PRAY TO GOD TO QUICKLY MAKE YOU WELL AND STRONG

FOR MY HEART IS LONGING FOR YOUR LOVE

NOW THAT YOU ARE GONE

SOON WE WILL BE TOGETHER OH HOW SPECIAL

OUR TIME WILL BE

IF YOU GET LONELY JUST GO TO SLEEP

THEN DREAM ABOUT ME

BECAUSE
OF
YOU

THINGS WERE NOT GOING AS WELL

AS I WANTED THEM TOO

BECAUSE OF YOUR HELP MY PLANS AND DREAMS

WILL HAVE A CHANCE TO BECOME TRUE

I JUST WANT TO SAY THANKS FOR HELPING

ME MAKE IT THROUGH

EVERYTHING WILL BE ALL RIGHT AND RUN SMOOTH

JUST BECAUSE OF YOU

SOON

OH_____ HOW GOOD OF A FRIEND

YOU HAVE BEEN

ALL I THINK ABOUT IS THE GOOD TIMES BACK THEN

HOW I WISH I COULD BE WITH YOU SOMETIMES

BUT THEN YOU ARE WITH ME IN HEART AND MIND

MAYBE SOMEDAY SOON WE WILL BE TOGETHER

THEN OUR FRIENDSHIP

CAN TURN TO LOVE AND LAST FOREVER

BABY
LOVE

IF I HAD MY CHOICE IN LIFE

I WOULD MAKE LOVE TO EVERY WOMAN IN SIGHT

I WOULD PLEASED THEM LONG AND SMOOTH

THEY COULD NEVER FORGET THE WAY I SOOTHE

I WOULD KISS THEM FROM HEAD TO TOE

MAKING THEM WAIT EVEN IF THEY

ARE READY TO FLOW

TAKING MY TIME TO MAKE THEM FEEL

WEAK AND COMPLETE

KNOWING WHEN I'M FINISHED THEY ARE UNABLE

TO GET TO THEIR FEET

READY TO PLEASE ANY WOMAN ANY TIME

THIS IS BABY LOVE WORKING HIS RHYME

PLEASANTLY

PLUMP

THERE'S A YOUNG LADY I MET TODAY

IT MIGHT BE ILLEGAL FOR ME TO BE FEELING THIS WAY

LOOKING AT HER YOU MIGHT SAY

SHE'S PLEASANTLY PLUMP

WHEN I LOOK AT HER ALL I DO IS

THINK ABOUT THAT RUMP

SHE HAS BIG BROWN SEXY BABY DOLL EYES

MAKING ME WANT TO CLIMB

IN BETWEEN THOSE THIGHS

WHEN SHE SMILES YOU WILL WANT TO SMILE BACK

ALL I BE THINKING IS HOW IS SHE IN THE SACK

THIS FINE SWEET LADY HAS TREATED ME KIND

BUT ALL I WANT TO DO IS KNOCK HER BOOTS ONE TIME

YOU MIGHT SAY I'M A NO GOOD CHUMP

BUT I KNOW I'VE GOT TO HAVE

SOME OF THAT PLEASANTLY PLUMP

FULL
MOON   RISING

THE GRAVITATIONAL FORCE OF THE SUN
CAUSES THE EARTH TO TURN AROUND AND AROUND
EVERYONE KNOWS THAT GRAVITY STOPS US FROM
FLOATING IN SPACE KEEPING OUR FEET ON THE GROUND
THE GRAVITATIONAL FORCE OF THE MOON IS A POWER
THAT SHOULD BE RECOGNIZED
IT HAS AN EFFECT ON THE BODY AND MIND
THIS YOU SHOULD KNOW AND REALIZE
THE FULL MOON HAS BEEN KNOWN TO CAUSE
HUNDRED FOOT TIDAL WAVES
IT HAS BEEN DOCUMENTED THAT IT SOMETIMES
SENT PEOPLE INTO A DESTRUCTIVE CRAZE
WEREWOLVES HAVE BEEN A FOLKLORE IN OUR COUNTRY
FOR MANY OF YEARS
DOCTORS AND NURSES WILL TELL YOU SOMETIMES
THE RESULTS OF A FULL MOON BRINGS THEM TO TEARS
THE VIOLENCE THEY SEE IN THE HOSPITAL IS DEVASTATING
DURING THIS PERIOD OF TIME
SCIENTIST SEARCH TO UNDERSTAND
THE EFFECT OF THE FULL MOON ON THE MIND
TO ALL OF YOU WHO DON'T BELIEVE
YOU BETTER BEWARE AND SOON
TIME IS APPROACHING THE END OF THE MONTH
THERE WILL BE A FULL MOON

LETS

CELEBRATE

MAY THIS DAY FILL YOU WITH JOY AND DELIGHT

MAY YOUR DAY BE OH SO HAPPY AND BRIGHT

FOR YOU DESERVE IT TO CONTINUE ON

FOR THIS IS THE DAY THAT YOU WERE BORN

LET LOVE PEACE AND HAPPINESS SHINE YOUR WAY

LET THE CELEBRATION BEGIN WITH A HAPPY BIRTHDAY

VICTORY

THE WORK WAS TOUGH BUT YOU DID ENOUGH

YOU STUDIED LONG AND GOT NOTHING WRONG

WORKING YOUR BODY AND MIND PUTTING IN THE TIME

I'M PROUD TO SAY THAT THIS IS YOUR DAY

CONGRATULATION ON YOUR TRIUMPHANT GRADUATION

KEEP   GOING

365 DAYS HAS COME AND GONE

THE MEMORY OF THE LAST ONE STILL LINGERS ON

NO ONE DOES IT LIKE YOU DO

SO I WISH A HAPPY BIRTHDAY TO YOU

LOVELY

ONCE AGAIN THIS MOMENTOUS OCCASION HAS COME

IT'S TIME TO GIVE A SPECIAL THANKS

TO A VERY SPECIAL SOMEONE

OH SO SWEET CARING AND FULL OF UNCONDITIONAL LOVE

SHARING IT WITH EVERYONE YOU GREET

REMINDING ME OF A BEAUTIFUL DOVE

THE DAY THAT YOU WERE BORN WAS

THE BEGINNING OF HAPPINESS FOR OH SO MANY

EVEN NOW THE LOVE THAT YOU GIVE

IS SEEMINGLY OH SO PLENTY

I THANK GOD FOR THE LOVE YOU SO

KINDLY DIRECTED MY WAY

I WANT YOU TO CELEBRATE AND HAVE AN

ENJOYABLE HAPPY BIRTHDAY

VISUALIZE

DESTINY FOR ME OH HOW I WISH THAT I COULD SEE

WHATEVER IT SHALL BE I MUST FACE ITS REALITY

LOOKING THROUGH THIS LOOKING GLASS

TO SEE MYSELF AT LAST

LEARNING TO FORGET THE PAST I MUST MOVE ON IN CLASS

TIME HAS COME AROUND UNDERSTANDING MUST BE FOUND

THINKING MUST BE SOUND NEVER LETTING MY HEAD DOWN

FOR MY PRECIOUS REALITY I'M FINALLY ABLE TO SEE

ALL THAT IT SHALL BE IT SHALL ONLY BE FOR ME

126

I Want To Say

Thanks To Everyone

For Your

Blessed Support

And

Inspirations

Made in the USA
San Bernardino, CA
31 March 2016